The Wardroom

An Officer's Tour at Sea
and the
Crisis of the US Navy

Thibaut Delloue

Micro Publishing Media
Stockbridge, MA 01262

The Wardroom: An Officer's Tour at Sea and the Crisis of the US Navy
Copyright © 2022 Thibaut F. Delloue

Printed in the United States of America

ISBN: 978-1-953321-20-6

MICRO PUBLISHING MEDIA, INC

Micro Publishing Media, Inc
PO Box 1522
Stockbridge, MA 01262

Table of Contents

Author's note: This book is an account of real events; however, many of the names of the individuals involved have been changed.

Note on spelling: Members of the Navy tend to use idiosyncratic spelling and capitalization for nautical terms. Throughout this book I spell words as closely to the conventional, non-Navy way as possible.

About the author: Thibaut Delloue hails from the great state of New Hampshire and served for five years as a surface warfare officer in the US Navy. He was the communications officer aboard the destroyer USS *Carney* and the navigator of the littoral combat ship USS *Coronado*. He completed his active-duty service in 2020.

"For upon a frigate's quarter-deck, it is not enough to sport a coat fashioned by a Stultz; it is not enough to be well braced with straps and suspenders; it is not enough to have sweet reminiscences of Lauras and Matildas. It is a right down life of hard wear and tear, and the man who is not, in a good degree, fitted to become a common sailor will never make an officer. Take that to heart, all ye naval aspirants. Thrust your arms up to the elbow in pitch and see how you like it, ere you solicit a warrant. Prepare for white squalls, living gales and typhoons; read accounts of shipwrecks and horrible disasters; peruse the Narratives of Byron and Bligh; familiarise yourselves with the story of the English frigate Alceste and the French frigate Medusa. Though you may go ashore, now and then, at Cadiz and Palermo; for every day so spent among oranges and ladies, you will have whole months of rains and gales."

—Herman Melville

Introduction

On a June evening in 2017, the warship USS *Fitzgerald* glided slowly into her pier in Yokosuka, Japan. The US Navy destroyer was returning sooner than expected—she had sailed out of this very port only the day before.

A spectator would have immediately noticed something was wrong. The *Fitzgerald* was pulled by two tugboats and leaned so noticeably that part of her stern normally below the waterline was visible. A large section of the steel frame on her starboard side was entirely caved in and hoses on her deck pumped water continuously over the side. The *Fitzgerald* looked like she had been hit by a missile. What any spectator could have not seen, however, was the gigantic gash in her hull below the water, behind which was a flooded compartment that caused the ship's severe list.

As sailors on the *Fitzgerald* threw mooring lines onto the pier, a team of US Navy divers readied themselves to enter the hole in her hull. The details of how the ship had been ripped open were still murky, though news agencies around the world were already reporting that the *Fitzgerald* had collided with a cargo ship off the coast of Japan and that seven of her sailors were missing. What the divers *did* know was that they would be searching for the bodies of these seven sailors.

At the same time the USS *Fitzgerald* limped back into port, I was aboard another destroyer, the USS *Carney*, somewhere in the Mediterranean Sea and was nearing the end of my first tour in the Navy as a surface warfare officer. When the news of the collision reached our ship, none of the *Carney's* sailors dared say aloud that the *Fitzgerald's* seven missing sailors were dead. None imagined that such a staggering loss of life could occur in peacetime aboard a warship identical to our own and that it would not be caused by a terrorist attack or a foreign military. Worse still, no one could have predicted that it would happen again.

Only two months later, the destroyer USS *John S. McCain* collided with a tanker while entering the Strait of Malacca near Singapore. In an eerie twist of fate, the impact left a hole in her hull that flooded a berthing space full of sleeping sailors, killing ten. Both incidents were two of the worst maritime disasters in recent memory.

For months afterward, we quietly wondered in our wardroom how the collisions of the *Fitzgerald* and the *McCain* unfolded. But by the time the investigations were over and the Navy released its final report, the media had more or less moved on from the tragedies and the American public never received an answer as to why seventeen sailors lost their lives while their ships conducted entirely routine transits that even non-Navy ships carried out in the world's oceans every day. To answer that question, I have to tell you what's it like to be a surface warfare officer and how some of the cracks in our community directly contributed to two of the most tragic events in the history of the American military.

From 2015 to 2017, I served aboard the Navy destroyer USS *Carney*. During my tour our ship sailed across the Atlantic and the waters of Europe from the English Channel to the eastern edge of the Mediterranean Sea. Our crew tailed Russian submarines, rescued migrants, fought ISIS in Libya, and moored in dozens of foreign ports. As her communications officer, I wrangled a small band of information systems technicians inside a cramped radio room and learned the subtleties of leadership, or at least how to coax people not to entirely lose their minds. At sea for most of these two years, *Carney* became a trying tour for everyone on board. I spent much of that time on the bridge learning the mariner's trade, which involved some terrifying moments and, in between, a lot of staring at water and finding novel ways to stay awake. Life at sea was stressful, slow, unforgiving, but also enormously rewarding.

This book is not just an account of that time. You would quickly become bored if it was, as there's only so much I can say about staring at the open ocean. This is not a story about war, and there are no Medals of Honor or grand firefights to recount. Navy ships have not been in combat for a long time and may not be for a long time still. Perhaps that's why we don't often see books or movies about the modern Navy. It's rather dull being out to sea, after all. It's also not the memoir of a retired admiral—there are perhaps a few leadership lessons here and there, but I wouldn't take it all too seriously.

This is a story about a few exciting moments and a lot of frustrating ones. It's partly my own story, but more importantly it's about the Surface Navy and the world of surface warfare officers, or "SWOs." There is not just one Navy, and the surface warfare community inhabits its own universe with its own peculiar rules and customs. I wrote this book because our culture is highly insular and does not reveal itself very easily. I always found it nearly impossible to explain to my family and friends back home what I did as a surface warfare officer. Hopefully this will help.

Much of my experience as a naval officer is no different from what the Navy has always been. It's not natural for humans to live on ships, and as much as sailors tend to fall in love with the ocean, going out to sea never loses a certain sense of loneliness. You are never alone on a naval vessel, but you cannot escape the dread of seeing only water or the same steel grey insides of a ship, every day for months at a time. The Navy is unforgiving by its very nature; it has always been, because there is no amount of technology or modern comforts that can make going out to sea for long periods of time not fundamentally suck.

SWOs have a rather loose job description in the Navy. They are the officers who serve aboard warships and oversee divisions of engineers, gunners, technicians, or any of the many jobs that make a naval vessel run. One thing all SWOs have in common, however, is that they stand watch on the bridge, the place where sailors drive and navigate a ship. They also follow the same career path: any SWO that remains in the Navy aims ultimately to command one of these ships.

Though the Navy is a hallowed institution in our country, it remains a government organization and, as such, is not without its dysfunctions. In fact, like a lot of government organizations, the Navy does not tend to do things in an especially effective or sensible manner. Being a SWO often felt more like being a bureaucrat than a warfighter, our lives ruled by endless manuals, regulations, meetings, and paperwork. As one senior chief petty officer I served with so bluntly put it, the Navy prepares its sailors for inspections, not war.

When I was in the Navy it seemed that almost every junior officer around me couldn't wait to get out. To be fair we had been warned: The SWO community had a famously poor reputation among other naval officers, even among enlisted sailors who had caught a glimpse of their wardroom's dynamics. The typical surface warfare officer, I was told from the very beginning, was overworked, undertrained, and deeply unsatisfied. The SWO community was rampant with horror stories, in no small part because every former SWO liked to claim they had it worse, about insane working hours, lack of sleep, and overbearing leadership. I knew that when I signed up to be a SWO, but wasn't the military *supposed* to be hard?

Nonetheless, it seemed something wasn't quite right with our organization, and in my five years of service I had the same conversation numerous times with other naval officers, and sometimes even my captains, in which we discussed the mystery of why things just couldn't seem to function normally in the Navy. Many of these sailors had never held any other job, but even they surmised that this was not how one of our military branches and a nearly two and a half centuries old institution was supposed to be run.

In 2017, the *Fitzgerald* and *McCain* tragedies brought these dysfunctions to the surface. The Navy's culture of institutional thinking had severely eroded our sailors' capabilities as mariners and warfighters. Our leaders, those in charge of our ships, our squadrons, and our fleets, seemed to care more about numbers on spreadsheets than they did about people. Though the collisions resulted in minor changes to the surface warfare community, for the most part the Navy was content to place the blame on a few high-ranking officers and, more tellingly, on the ships themselves. The fallout failed to bring about the reckoning that the Surface Navy desperately called for: a complete rethinking of the way surface officers are trained and the dismantling of our toxic work culture. Somewhere along the last few decades, the Navy's leadership has seemingly forgotten that surface officers, above all else, ought to be mariners and warfighters.

But let's start from the beginning—before all that I was a civilian and I didn't know anything at all about ships.

CHAPTER 1

"Don't Lose Your Minds!"

As far back as I can remember, I always wanted to join the military. I suppose all boys do at some point, but for me that feeling never went away. I was eleven years old on September 11. Our teachers broke the news to us at the end of a school day, though it wasn't until I got home and saw the Twin Towers crumbling on television that I realized something terrible had happened. I came of age during the War on Terror, when images of American soldiers patrolling the desert and leveling Middle Eastern cities were commonplace in the media. It was a time of renewed patriotic fervor in the country. Everywhere you looked men and women in uniform were paraded about and we were constantly thanking people for their service. One day a Marine recruiter visited my high school and nearly convinced me to enlist. He called my house several times, and my mother was horrified. Instead, while other Americans my age were going off to war, I did the sensible thing and went to college.

But the idea of military service lingered, and although I wish I did it for more selfless reasons, the truth is I joined the military, like many others, because I thought it would be pretty damn cool to be thanked for *my* service. There is not much else that you can get thanked for, unless you want to be a doctor or something, and that seemed like it wasn't as much fun. So sometime after graduating, on a blisteringly cold New England day, I walked into a nondescript government building in Boston and timidly found my way to the Navy's regional officer recruiting station. A lieutenant in the now extinct blue camouflage uniform sailors wore at the time sat me down and asked me right away what job I wanted to do. At that time, I knew very little about the Navy but I knew I wanted to be on a ship. That's why I had decided to join the Navy to begin with. I grew up near the New Hampshire seacoast and loved the ocean and the romantic notion of going out to sea and standing watch on the bridge of a warship. My dad had been a submariner in the French Navy and my grandfather before him had been a Navy man. Joining the Navy is not like joining the infantry services. Sailors, though we like to say we are warfighters, don't really go into combat anymore. No—for me, the Navy had its own unique draw. This was the seagoing service, and, I imagined, the most gentlemanly of all the military branches.

I told him I wanted to be a surface warfare officer, even though at the time I had only a vague notion of what that meant. "Being a SWO sucks," he told me immediately. "I mean, it can be great. I know guys who are SWOs that are tearing it up on riverboats in Florida" (this would turn out to be a totally false statement), "but I also know guys that freakin' hate it and if they're not working twelve-hour days in port, then they're out to sea and working twenty-four hours a day. So if you want to be a SWO I won't stop you, but if I were you I'd be an aviator." Well, I wore glasses so being a Navy pilot was out of the question. "You can still be an NFO," he assured me. "A naval flight officer. They are the guys who sit in the backseat of an aircraft and operate the radar and the weapons systems. The copilot."

I had never had any desire to be an aviator. I didn't care for the long training or the bomber jacket, nor did I want to sit for hours inside a cramped cockpit while, in this case, somebody else got to drive. Unfortunately, at that time the Navy wasn't hiring SWOs. I had missed my chance for the Naval Academy and instead was applying for Officer Candidate School, a twelve-week training program for college graduates and the Navy's way to fill gaps in officer billets.

Eventually the lieutenant sold me on the NFO idea. "Look, you know what the two coolest jobs in the world are? Rock star and pilot. They make movies out of those jobs. Well, you can't be a pilot, but you can be the copilot. You ever seen *Top Gun*? You'd be Goose. From *Top Gun*." That was a winning argument for a guy in his twenties, so I put NFO on my list, and because I thought the Navy was booked with SWOs I eagerly awaited my new life as Goose from *Top Gun*. I still put SWO as the number one choice on my application. Just in case.

Nearly a year later, I was finally accepted into Officer Candidate School and, better still, I got what I wanted. The less rock and roll but more romantic option: surface warfare officer. I returned to the recruiting office to raise my right hand and swear the oath of enlistment. There was no turning back now.

Years later, I am standing watch on the bridge of a warship on a frigid winter night in the Black Sea, staring at darkness and an empty radar screen. It crosses my mind that I should have listened to my recruiter. Maybe I should have been an aviator.

The Navy's Officer Candidate School, or OCS, is tucked away in a corner of Naval Station Newport inside Rhode Island's Narragansett Bay. For every branch of the military, OCS is the fast track to a commission as an officer: a three-month-long boot camp that indoctrinates raw candidates into the world of military discipline and customs. I arrived in Newport on a mild December day, clean-shaven and dressed in khaki trousers and a tucked-in polo shirt. I was directed to check in by members of the most senior class, dubbed "candidate officers," who were only a few weeks away from graduation. Candidates at OCS were divided into different phases of training, and I was at that point an "Indoctrination Candidate," or more simply, a civilian nonentity. I noticed all the other new arrivals had the same schoolboy outfit and dumbfounded look on their faces and together we looked like we were joining a cult.

Soon after our cell phones were taken away and our hair buzzed off. We then filled out a lot of paperwork and were issued an endless amount of *stuff*—uniform items, toiletries, classroom supplies—and piled it all as best we could into a green seabag. At some point during that first day the candidate officers sat us down in a classroom and laid down the ground rules for OCS: You will address everyone by a title, be it sir, ma'am, staff sergeant or gunnery sergeant, chief or senior chief, and candidate officer. You will stand or sit at the position of attention unless told to be at ease. You will move with a sense of urgency wherever you go, but never run unless told to do so. You will account for every item you are issued and not lose anything. You will not look your instructors in the eyeballs but keep your eyes straight ahead unless told otherwise. You will ask permission to use the restroom or to ask questions. You will not behave inappropriately, laugh or smile out of turn, or disrespect anyone. You will refer to things around you the Navy way: Walls are bulkheads, the ground is the deck, the ceiling is the overhead, restrooms are heads, windows are portholes, and the proper response to a question is either "yes," "no," or "aye aye." It was highly advisable to never say "I don't know." And most importantly, you will not lie, cheat, or steal. That, they warned us, was the surest ticket out of Newport.

We were assigned to rooms that we shared with one roommate. Though it was a relief we wouldn't live inside large berthings like in boot camp, we'd be responsible for keeping our rooms spotless and our beds made with military precision every day. My first roommate was a Southerner who had been accepted into the submarine program which, because it required long training on nuclear reactors, was the more competitive of the Navy's officer communities. He had been held back from a previous class for failing several fitness events, so had been in Newport for weeks before my arrival while he waited to rejoin training. He had, as a result, a surprising amount of knowledge about what I could expect over the next few weeks, and so turned out to be a rather useful roommate. He had also acquired a secret weapon: an alarm clock. These were forbidden during the first phase of OCS because candidates were supposed to be awoken by their instructors to induce stress from the very onset of training. Other candidates had gotten hold of alarm clocks, however, and devised a plan of knocking on each other's walls in the morning to get the next room to wake up before the official "reveille," or wake-up call. The walls were thick concrete, though, so their scheme came to nothing.

The candidate officers, nicknamed "Candi-Os" at OCS, spent the first few days teaching us basic military customs and courtesies and preparing us to meet our instructors. The real point of pride for naval officers who earn their commission through OCS is that we are trained primarily by Marine Corps drill instructors. Although there are also Navy instructors at OCS, the Corps' culture of toughness elevated our training to a considerable degree. Like the eternal Gunnery Sergeant Hartman in *Full Metal Jacket*, Marine drill instructors are legendary in our military and bring a whole other level of intensity and physical pain to Navy training. Naval officers who have gone through OCS like to hold this fact over graduates of the Naval Academy who get yelled at, strangely enough, by other midshipmen. The Candi-Os, although strict, were not drill instructors. They were there to prepare this timid group of college graduates for military indoctrination.

The real first day of training, the day we met our instructors, was known as "Wake Up Wednesday," and was the start of what was informally referred to as *fuck-fuck games*. The aim of military training is to induce stress to test how individuals cope with a wartime environment. Instructors invent arbitrary rules, set time limits for everything, and scream at you to make everyday tasks seem impossible. In the morning, for example, every candidate was expected to be standing outside their room at attention and ready for morning physical training, or PT, in a matter of seconds. That meant dressed, shoes laced, socks pulled up, and shirts tucked in. Part of that was a test of our forethought; it was impossible to wake up and dress in the amount of time allowed by the instructors. Instead we slept in the next day's uniform, socks included, and our shoes already laced. We could then roll out of bed, slip on our sneakers, and be outside our doors in seconds. One thing you did *not* want to do at OCS was be last at anything. Instructors were constantly on the lookout for *that* candidate, and being last out "on line" in the mornings guaranteed a very shitty start to your day.

The night before Wake Up Wednesday I barely slept. At 4 a.m., we were jolted awake by the banging and shouts of Navy chiefs and Marine sergeants outside our rooms. Within a few seconds nearly every candidate stood at attention, their eyes fixed forward, in two long lines on either side of the hallway. Those who took a little more time, who hadn't heeded the advice to sleep with their socks on or who just moved too slowly, met our drill instructor for the first time in a rather forceful fashion. Like wolves, drill instructors work better in packs; having just one in your face was one thing, but when a group pounced on you and screamed so close you could feel their spit, they *really* got their point across.

Our first day continued with a lot of *fuck-fuck games*: get on your face and do pushups, on your back for bicycle kicks, now on your feet and start pumping out squats. The point was to do everything fast and loud and obey orders quickly and without hesitation. If you got something wrong, if you didn't sound off, or if you were last, you'd get screamed at. The more Marines and Navy chiefs were in a candidate's face, the more you knew that person was screwing up.

We had entered the first phase of training, the indoctrination phase, where our days were split between physical training, classroom instruction on basic Navy subjects, and drill. When one ended, we speed-walked to the next in formation, clutching M16 rifles in the brutally cold winds of Narragansett Bay. If we were not sitting down in a classroom or at the mess hall, everything at OCS was done with speed and intensity. In the beginning, in fact, we quickly adjusted our understanding of what it meant to be fast or loud in the eyes of a Marine drill instructor.

Mealtimes required a complex set of maneuvers we referred to as "chow hall procedures." After stacking our rifles outside, we formed in front of the entrance and uniformly removed our coats, hats, and gloves while our instructors counted down and we shouted memorized maxims like the definition of *discipline* in unison (*"Discipline is the instant willing obedience to orders, respect for authority, and self-reliance!"*). If an instructor saw a single candidate move or an item of clothing out of place after the end of their countdown, or if our "ditties" were not recited in perfect speed and unison, the whole ritual would be repeated from the beginning. Two candidates then marched out of formation, swinging their arms and pivoting their bodies together, and opened the chow hall doors. The entire class began jogging in place, which we continued until the instructors were satisfied with our level of intensity, and the candidate in charge of the class that day, the section leader, poked their head into the mess hall and shouted, "Class 08-15 Charlie Company, filing in for chow!"

One by one candidates ran into the mess hall while yelling their number in sequence. We then sped through the chow line, holding our trays with elbows locked at a ninety-degree angle, and neatly filled our tables. We stood behind our chair and waited for the entire class to get their food, during which we held our candidate notebooks, filled with the general military knowledge and Navy gauge we were required to memorize while at OCS, with arms extended and "parallel to the deck." Everyone sat down and ate together, backs straight and feet together at the "position of attention," eyes forward, bringing food and drinks to our mouths and never the other way around.

If you screwed up this mealtime ritual, if you ate messily, or if God forbid you caught the eyes of a DI, you were quickly assaulted by instructors and it was likely you would not eat much that day. Chow hall procedures, other than to train us to follow directions and work as a team, were a way to put section leaders to the test. If the class messed up, it reflected on them. As time wore on and the instructors backed off and allowed the class to manage themselves more, we increasingly saw these procedures as a source of ridiculousness and even embarrassment. Officer candidates were not the only people who used the chow hall at Naval Station Newport, and I imagined it was more than bewildering for someone to see a band of fifty crazed maniacs running and shouting in unison while they tried to enjoy their food.

It wasn't until we reached the last stage of our training and we began preparing new candidates ourselves that we took up the insane ritual with renewed fervor, because now *we* could harangue others for screwing up at the chow hall. When I found myself on the other side of this little game, I realized how intimidated and small grown men and women could be made to feel in the face of authority, as I am sure I had been when in the new candidates' position weeks before. I will never forget a particularly meek indoctrination candidate in our class of trainees who, when I asked him why the items in front of him were messed up (his utensils were arranged in the wrong order), shouted, with eyes fixed forward and at the perfect position of attention, "Because it looks like *shit*, candidate officer!"

At least several hours of every day at OCS were taken up by rifle drill practice, which became for many the most dislikable part of training.

Sailors are not exactly known for their proficiency at military drill. We are, as a whole, not that physically fit, often undisciplined, and we rarely get a chance to put on a flashy uniform and show off on a parade deck. Those things are exactly what Marines are good at. Drilling with an eight-pound M16 became brutal after a few hours, as it quickly felt more like carrying a sledgehammer in front of your chest. The key to surviving drill sessions was to keep your rifle raised and not make any stupid faces when your arms started to hurt. That lack of discipline is exactly what our hawk-eyed drill instructor, Staff Sergeant Nichols, looked for. He doled out punishments for any misstep—"HIT THE GROUND AND START PUSHING!" or "RUN A LAP AROUND THE PARADE DECK!" If enough candidates were messing up, he'd order the entire class to hold our rifles in front of us with one hand until he was satisfied we'd learned our lesson. His favorite taunt was "don't lose your minds!" It became our class's unofficial catchphrase.

As we progressed, the repeat offenders increasingly drew his anger. There's a reason "drill" instructors earned that name—other than physical fitness, drill is the one thing they take very seriously. OCS classes held a drill competition during the fifth week, and being crowned champion was a title every Marine instructor competed for. Learning to wear our khaki uniforms and passing exams about navigation meant nothing to them compared to our competence as a drilling unit. Staff Sergeant Nichols claimed to hold the record for the highest drill competition score as a DI at Parris Island, where enlisted Marines are trained, and intended to uphold his reputation in Newport. So when some candidates repeatedly screwed up, he took it personally, and those were the times he unleashed his most furious tirades.

As the weeks wore on, we earned time to ourselves during the day to study for classes and ready our uniforms for inspections. The culminating event of the first phase of training was the Room, Locker, Personnel inspection, or RLP. While it would last no more than fifteen minutes, RLP came with strict guidelines on how to wear your uniform and arrange your gear, your furniture, and your room, down to the most minute details of how to fold and label your socks and the length of the fold of your bedsheets. A speck of dust on your mirror could make the difference between passing and failing. Instructors would also grill us on a long list of memorized knowledge about the military.

When the dreaded RLP finally came, I found myself on the wrong end of the hallway. Among the last to be tested, I stood for at least forty-five minutes at the perfect position of attention, back straight, fists closed with the thumb along the seam of my trousers, and eyes transfixed at the wall in front of me, while all around a maelstrom of noise erupted. While I was strictly forbidden from turning my head or even moving my eyes, I could hear instructors shouting orders, candidates screaming back in sheer terror, and objects being thrown inside rooms. Finally, and without warning, the mangled face of a Marine DI appeared about two inches from my own. "NAME ALL MARINE ENLISTED RANKS STARTING FROM PRIVATE!" he shouted. And so it began, as I answered at maximum volume while the DI began inspecting every inch of my uniform. "LOOSE THREAD, MINUS ONE ... BOOTS LOOK LIKE SHIT, MINUS ONE ..."

He directed me inside the room, where he ordered me to get on my face and start pumping out pushups while shouting verbatim descriptions of Navy warfare insignias. If it was clear I knew them, he cut me off and issued a new question. In the next room, I heard a candidate bellowing the Marines' Hymn. I had entered a personalized hell, where I alternated between furious exercises and screamed so loud for fifteen straight minutes that I expected my eyes to pop out of their sockets. Meanwhile, my instructor tore my room apart item by item, hurling neatly folded uniforms and toiletries over my head to break my concentration. "STREAK ON MIRROR, MINUS ONE ... BED FOLD DOESN'T MEASURE SIX INCHES, MINUS ONE ..."

Finally, after a brutal minute of rifle squats while listing Navy officer rank, he ordered me to return to the position of attention in the hallway. So ended RLP. Later, while we put our rooms back together (it looked like a tornado had run through our hallway) and eagerly recounted the chaos we had endured, those who had failed were individually approached by instructors. I was not one of them, which meant I had successfully passed the first, and arguably the most difficult, phase of training.

After the RLP inspection we entered the next phase of training and focus shifted to class-based knowledge and leadership indoctrination. We learned to wear dress uniforms and no longer had to shout during subsequent inspections. We got more time to ourselves to study and were, individually, given more responsibility in managing our class. Those who did not pass RLP got another chance, and if they failed again, they "rolled" to another class and repeated the previous three weeks of training. Those who failed for physical reasons, meanwhile, rolled into the holding class until they were fit enough to continue. Because of this, OCS was near impossible to fail, and despite it being no joke, its forgiving nature was one of its most puzzling features.

Most of the candidates who didn't commission, in fact, and this was a relatively small number, were dropped for ethics violations. A few were caught cheating on tests. One was caught lying down in an empty room trying to catch extra sleep during the day, not a violation worthy of expulsion by itself until he lied about it to instructors. Another was kicked out, and this was a story I would continue to recount for the rest of my Navy career, because during the first week of training he asked the servers at the mess hall for some chicken fajitas, but pronounced it with a long *i*, presumably because it sounded like "vagina," and because he thought that would be funny. It turned out the servers at the mess hall were special needs employees, and he was promptly shown the door.

But other than committing clear wrongdoings, simply being incompetent didn't seem to qualify as worthy of expulsion at OCS. I will mention here one notable example of this, a candidate who, because of a wrist injury, had been living in medical for nine months by the time he rolled into our class. He had been in Newport for so long, he told me, that he had bought a car with the salary he had earned. When he joined us, this candidate, I'll call him Garcia, was utterly unprepared for physical activity. He trudged through PT sessions, panting and wincing all the way, and earned the special disdain of Staff Sergeant Nichols, who made it a point not to allow this man to commission as a naval officer. Most inexcusable was that, after all those months with nothing to do but heal his wrist, Garcia didn't seem to know the first thing about the Navy or military discipline.

During our weeklong Christmas break, I attempted to help him study for the RLP inspection, when to my astonishment I realized he had not memorized any of the required knowledge in our candidate booklets. He seemed, in fact, to feel very little motivation in doing so, and there was not much more I could do to help him. Unsurprisingly he failed the inspection twice in a row and was rolled yet again to another class. It turned out Garcia did eventually earn his commission in the Navy, for over two years later, as I checked in to the Littoral Combat Ship squadron in San Diego following my first tour, I saw him roaming about with the same clueless expression on his face he had had in Newport. We made small talk but with a quick glance at his uniform I realized he had not earned his Surface Warfare pin during his first tour, which by now he would have inevitably completed. This squadron, I gathered, was his last holding place before he would, without a warfare pin, almost certainly be discharged from the Navy.

In the last phase of OCS we transitioned from "officer candidates" to "candidate officers," and it was now our job to prepare and train the incoming class for *their* first phase. After just over two months it was hard to believe the transformation we had undergone and that a short while ago *we* were the ones arriving in Newport for the first time. The instructors, during this phase, almost disappeared from view and let us manage the arrival of the incoming candidates ourselves and prepare them for Wake Up Wednesday. We now wore khaki service uniforms every day, which was wholly inadequate for piles of snow and subfreezing temperatures. For a week we wrangled our group of new candidates around base as we taught them military basics that we ourselves had learned only weeks before. This was our first taste of authority in the military, and as such the candidate officers kept each other in check lest one of us veered off into a power trip. Just as we had quivered under the authority of *our* candidate officers, our trainees were utterly convinced that we occupied some exalted position. We had to remind ourselves that we were not drill instructors and were certainly not yet naval officers.

My roommate and close friend at OCS, Stuart, offered a crucial piece of advice before the end of our training. For the previous five years he had been an enlisted Seabee, a specialized corps of the Navy whose name comes from the acronym for their official title as the Navy's "Construction Battalions" (CB). These are a hybrid of construction worker and infantryman who build military installations in combat areas. Stuart had deployed in Afghanistan and had risen through the enlisted ranks very quickly. At OCS it was not uncommon to see candidates who, put into a leadership position for the first time in their young lives, quickly demonstrated they did not understand the line between humility and arrogance. Stuart, on the other hand, was one of the calmest and most level-headed guys among us. Despite his vastly superior knowledge of the Navy, he only said his piece when he felt it was absolutely needed.

Stuart told me one night: "In the military you can't just show up and start ordering people around. It doesn't matter that you're an officer. You have to *build a rapport with them first.* You have to show them at least you know what you're talking about, that you're worthy of leading them. Otherwise your guys will let on they respect you, they will salute you and call you 'sir,' but when your back is turned they won't hesitate to talk shit about you." Later on in my Navy career I saw officers who couldn't stomach it when enlisted sailors showed them any disrespect and who would go off and complain that Petty Officer So-And-So had been curt with them that morning. Stuart's point served me well: regardless of your rank in the Navy, when you are new it is best to use your head before you immediately climb on your high horse.

Shortly before commissioning day the would-be Surface Warfare Officers in my class chose their first ships. Every SWO must serve two tours at sea as division officers, each lasting two years, during their initial enlistment. Our list of ships was a stroke of good luck, with spots open for ships in San Diego, Hawaii, Japan, and Spain. Almost all of us got what we wanted, and I jumped on the opportunity to head to Rota, Spain, one of the most sought-after duty stations in the Navy. A small military installation in southern Spain, near the Strait of Gibraltar, Naval Base Rota is jointly run by the Spanish and US Navies. I was lucky that two new destroyers would be moving there that year to bolster American presence in the Mediterranean Sea. I chose the USS *Carney*, DDG 64, an *Arleigh Burke*-class guided-missile destroyer that, though at the time still homeported in Mayport, Florida, would soon be making the voyage to Spain.

In March, after twelve weeks locked inside an island in Newport, we put on our dress blues and commissioned as ensigns in the US Navy. Though it was a momentous event for us all, I also realized that the single gold band around my sleeve would not mean much in the real fleet, which was nothing like basic training. I could take solace, however, in the fact that I would never have to do rifle drill ever again.

CHAPTER 2

505 Feet of American Fighting Steel

After commissioning day and a week of leave, I immediately headed to Norfolk, Virginia, to attend Basic Division Officers Course, or BDOC, the initial training for all first-tour surface officers. BDOC, at the time, was eight weeks of learning a little about everything and, consequently, not very much about anything at all. It became my introduction to the Navy method of instruction, otherwise known as "death by PowerPoint," which rests on the assumption that if you sit in a classroom and are bombarded with information all day, enough of it will stick to make you qualified in *something*. BDOC, for that reason, mostly flew over our heads. It didn't focus on anything in particular but glanced over several aspects of shipboard life: engineering, communications, navigation, and the complicated Navy bureaucracy. Because we only spent a handful of classes on any of these, we walked away probably more unsure of ourselves than when we started.

Our instructors were shore duty lieutenants who had just completed their initial sea tours and had little motivation to expend extra effort on clueless ensigns. For two months we sat idly as they read PowerPoint slides to us and explained carefully what parts of these to remember to pass exams. Wedged between these classes were a handful of simulator sessions that offered a basic introduction to driving ships: how to give standard engine and rudder orders to a helmsman on the bridge, and how not to crash into other vessels on a collision course. It was clear that the BDOC curriculum was still a work in progress and served only as a haphazard introduction to the Surface Navy. Established only a few years before, BDOC had been hastily cobbled together after concerns grew over a complete lack of formal training for surface warfare officers in the Navy.

The instructors at BDOC made it clear that our first tours were going to suck. Though we had graduated from OCS with plenty of pride in our commissions, we quickly realized that in the real Navy being an unqualified ensign meant very little. Although enlisted sailors, even senior enlisted chiefs with twenty years in the Navy, saluted you, there was an implicit understanding that you knew nothing, at least not yet, and that your title as an officer was in name only. Our leadership courses at OCS and BDOC emphasized the difference between positional leadership, what we had by virtue of our rank, and *actual* leadership. Being an officer would not earn us immediate respect from our sailors. Even at the time I failed to understand why prospective surface warfare officers, unlike pilots or any other community in the Navy, were sent to their first duty station with little knowledge, no technical skills, and no real experience. That seemed like a backward system even to a totally green sailor like me. I trusted that the Navy had a reason for this, however, and that it would never let unqualified people run divisions, or worse, drive ships at sea.

I graduated from BDOC in June and subsequently made the nine-hour drive to Mayport, Florida, where the USS *Carney* was then still stationed and awaiting her homeport shift. That is, incidentally, probably the least interesting nine-hour drive in America—at some point you start to see palm trees and realize you are getting close. When I got to base, I changed right away into my dress blues and was picked up by my sponsor, Mike, one of the officers on the *Carney* whose role would be to guide me into the complex world I was about to enter. That transition is daunting for any new sailor, even an officer, and on my first real day in the Navy I was glad to have Mike alongside me as I walked onto a Navy ship for the first time, with only one thin gold band on my sleeve and a single ribbon on my uniform. It is not an uncommon mistake, in fact, for new sailors to stroll onto the wrong ship altogether just because she has the same hull number as the one they've been assigned to.

Mike gave me a few pointers as we passed through the security gate for the pier: "When you step onto a Navy ship, you should stop at the end of the brow, turn and salute the ensign [the flag flying at the very stern of the ship while in port], then salute the OOD and request permission to come aboard, since it's your first time here." In port the officer of the deck, or OOD, acts as the ship's security guard. Enlisted sailors request permission to come on board or go ashore, but officers assigned to a ship simply report their arrival or departure. I got a scowl and a curt salute from the chief standing watch at the time, because the last thing that chief wanted was another clueless ensign to train, and stepped on board.

From the outside, I was awestruck by the *Carney's* sleek lines and intimidating form. *This* was a warship, and the very reason why I had joined the Navy. As an *Arleigh Burke*-class "destroyer," a name derived from WWI-era "torpedo boat destroyers," the *Carney* was among the Navy's most versatile and capable vessels. She was equipped with torpedoes, long-range artillery, machine guns, embarked helicopters, and almost a hundred missiles capable of taking down aircraft and submarines and striking land targets nearly one thousand miles away. Destroyers have long been dubbed the "Cadillacs of the sea," and for good reason. With her four powerful gas turbine engines, the *Carney* could achieve speeds of well over thirty knots and, equipped with rotating propeller blades, was capable of stopping and reversing on a dime. She was also loaded with antennas, sensors, radars, a bow-mounted sonar, and a towed array (nicknamed the "tail") that could detect submarines in the water.

Though she was two decades old, the *Carney* remained a reliable, powerful warship that could serve multiple roles, from escorting carriers to sailing alone in the world's most remote waters. Her unofficial motto, proudly displayed on banners and crew T-shirts, was fitting: "505 feet of American fighting steel."

After stepping aboard, Mike led me to the administrative office to check in with the ships' yeomen. I sat there awkwardly in my dress blues, meeting sailors as they walked by the office. New ensigns don't evoke much reaction out of a ship's crew and are mostly something to ignore. Who wants to follow orders from someone who's "been in the Navy since breakfast," as the saying goes? I was well aware of that, of course, and that, despite the single gold band on my sleeves, I wouldn't be taken very seriously until I proved myself among the ship's crew. I also knew that as an officer reporting to his ship my most important meeting would be with my captain; that was one first impression I did not want to get wrong. Luckily he poked his head into the administrative office as I sat there dumbfounded, waiting for the yeomen to process my paperwork.

Commander Ben Pinckney, *Carney's* commanding officer, was not exactly what I expected when I thought of a ship's captain. Small and rotund, though not exactly fat, his diminutive figure was made worse by a high-pitched, nasally voice and a head speckled with so little hair as to be nearly bald. As a prior-enlisted sailor who commissioned well into his Navy career, he was easily the oldest member of the crew and older than most officers his rank. Mike introduced me, and Pinckney eyed me so as to size up his newest junior officer. "Welcome aboard," he said. "You're probably going to be the commo. Your job sucks." He did not shake my hand or ask any questions, and so ended my first meeting with my first commanding officer. I would come to learn he was not exaggerating.

"Commo" stood for communications officer, one of the many abbreviations given to officers aboard Navy ships. Among others, the *Carney's* gunnery officer was dubbed "gunno," her supply officer "suppo," and her weapons officer "weps." One of my first challenges, then, was to navigate the labyrinthian world of Navy terms and acronyms. These didn't just end with the traditional maritime lexicon, where left and right were port and starboard, walls were bulkheads, the floor was the deck, the ceiling was the overhead, and bathrooms were "heads." Sailors' vocabulary contained an endless list of outlandish words which, at first, sounded like an entirely different language.

After this rather ominous meeting with the skipper, I met the communications officer I'd be replacing, Melissa. Mike handed me off quickly, probably glad to be rid of the new ensign, and Melissa rushed me through the ship's passageways to meet with the sailors who would make up my division. On my first day on a Navy ship, however, it was highly inadvisable to refer to anything as "mine," as sailors don't start out with much confidence in fresh-faced division officers.

On the inside, *Carney* was a daunting, unwelcoming labyrinth. It took me weeks to figure out which way was forward and aft or port and starboard, and that's when I didn't confuse what port and starboard meant. I would often wander the ship's long grey passageways, peeking through watertight doors into cramped spaces and wondering what lay inside. Most of my efforts during the first few days on board, in fact, were taken up trying to find my own workspace and berthing.

That first day, I followed Melissa out of the administrative office as she effortlessly navigated through passageways and down ladder wells, past twisted pipes and cables and firefighting equipment hanging from bulkheads. More than one bruise was incurred as I slammed my head into scuttle openings or my shins into hatches (which is why the bottom part of a hatch is called a "knee knocker" and often has to be repainted). After descending several ladder wells into a narrow vestibule, we arrived in front of a heavy steel door adorned with warnings like "SECRET" and "DO NOT ENTER WITHOUT AUTHORIZATION." Melissa punched in a code and opened the door. This was the radio room, and it was inhabited by the information systems technicians, or simply ITs, who were, for lack of a better term, the *Carney's* geek squad.

Colloquially known as "radio," their workspace was a cramped maze lined with radio transceivers, network hardware, and encryption boxes. It was the ITs' job to keep these machines working, a momentous responsibility for teenagers and twenty-somethings with little formal training. This, however, is the norm in the Navy, where near-high schoolers are quickly converted into technical experts. I shook a few hands and was met with a few wary looks from the ITs, as enlisted sailors generally approach new officers with suspicion.

But Melissa didn't have time to introduce me to the complexities of radio. "Our department head wants to meet you," she explained. "I should warn you, though, he's got a bit of a *reputation* around here." Luckily my new direct supervisor and department head, Lieutenant Masker, worked only two decks directly above the radio room.

Lieutenant Masker was Carney's combat systems officer, or CSO, and was the third-highest-ranking officer on board the ship. I met him inside his stateroom, which served as both his office and bedroom, and after a cold handshake, sat down for our first one-on-one. Broad-shouldered and physically imposing, Masker possessed a dark face that rarely disclosed any emotion other than impatience, and occasionally sheer anger. After some brief small talk, he stared at me for a moment and told me that, when I actually turned over as the communications officer, I had better be ready to "hit the ground running." The ship was in the middle of her training phase and was gearing up for a three-week transit across the Atlantic, a homeport shift, and a four-month deployment. "I need you to learn your job quickly," he explained curtly. "When it comes to radio, I'll be asking you and you only. Not your chief. Not your petty officers. *You're* in charge down there." He had little patience, he noted, for the "ensign salute." Masker had been an enlisted medic before joining the officer side of the Navy and gave little leeway to OCS-trained officers, despite their brief training. He was also possessed by an uncompromising, *get-shit-done* attitude. If I didn't understand something, I was expected to figure it out quickly and on my own. If he asked for something, it had better get done regardless of whether I knew what it was he even wanted. Lieutenant Masker wasn't in the habit of explaining the same thing twice.

He also appeared to be permanently incensed with everyone around him, like he had given up on humanity a long time ago and expected nothing but disappointment from us. Despite his placid exterior, it seemed like he could burst from his chair and start choking someone at any moment. Nonetheless he rarely raised his voice and intimidated junior officers simply with his icy death stare. Most people, enlisted or officer, did not talk to Lieutenant Masker unless they had to and unfortunately, because he was my direct boss, I had to speak to him every single day. During his year-long tenure as my department head, Masker never once inquired about my personal life. I don't think he even learned my first name.

Melissa then led me around the corner from Masker's stateroom to the wardroom, the officers' mess on a Navy ship. Ostensibly the place where officers eat and relax, the wardroom also acts as a default location for meetings and work conversations. Because it's the central place where officers gather, the term *wardroom* also refers to a ship's officers in general.

As the first among a wave of new ensigns that would join the *Carney* before her move to Spain, I was unequivocally the new guy and the de facto source of amusement for not knowing the endless traditions and courtesies that accompanied shipboard life. I did not realize, for example, that we were to request permission from the senior officer present in the wardroom before we sat down at the table, or that two chairs were reserved there exclusively for the captain and the executive officer. I broke these rules immediately upon entering the wardroom that first day. The latter was especially inexcusable since those two chairs were marked with bright gold letters reading *CO* and *XO*. Despite my embarrassment, I quickly realized that making sport of new ensigns was a hallowed Navy tradition in itself.

After meeting some of the *Carney's* junior officers, who playfully promised that being a SWO wasn't as daunting as it now appeared, Melissa handed me off to another officer who escorted me down several decks and through the entire length of the ship to my berthing. Though most officers earned the right to live inside staterooms with only one to three beds, nearly all the first-tour male ensigns, and we were for the most part male, lived together in a cramped berthing space well below the waterline and nearly at the aft end of the ship. From there it was a long walk to the bridge, especially when we woke up in the middle of the night to stand watch. As the exclusive domain of male junior officers, our berthing was named the "JO Jungle" aboard the *Carney*. It was here that over a dozen of us slept, lounged, and shared a single toilet and shower. I was introduced to my "rack," a narrow bed that I could barely lie straight inside of, with thin curtains to close out the light and noise outside. These were stacked three on top of one another and could be lifted to reveal small sections of storage which, along with a tiny locker, made up the whole of our "personal space" on the *Carney*.

I was finally left alone to explore my living arrangements, feeling entirely dejected and out of my element. I knew a SWO's first tour wasn't supposed to be easy, but I couldn't fathom how I would, in a few months, get underway and balance standing watch, managing a division, and keeping up with my qualifications all at once. I was also hearing horror stories from the crew about the ship's schedule. My boss, it seemed, hadn't been lying. "I hope you're not looking to spend any time on land during this tour!" one of the officers had told me in the wardroom. I had arrived exactly as *Carney* would enter a heavy operational cycle, and would, in the next two years, spend considerably more time at sea than tied to a pier. Meanwhile, my friends from Officer Candidates School who joined as prospective aviators were still sitting comfortably in classrooms at Pensacola, years away from even entering the fleet. I began to understand why the Surface Navy had such a difficult reputation. As I sat on my rack and pondered my predicament, I also realized I had no idea how to navigate my way back to radio, the wardroom, or even the ship's exit, of which at that point I didn't know how many there were.

My first days on the *Carney* were spent following Melissa around and trying to get a handle on my future responsibilities. She introduced me as best she could to the convoluted world of Navy communications, with its circuits, antennas, servers, networks, satellites, and how all these fit together. Sailors use the term PFM to describe how this complex web actually works, which stands for "pure fucking magic."

One of my primary responsibilities as commo would be to manage the ship's cryptographic keys and the equipment used to encode and decode radio circuits and networks. The crypto manager is the most hated responsibility for any junior officer. As my second captain on the *Carney* liked to remind me, "There are two people on this ship who can land me in jail: One is the supply officer, the other is you." The Navy's communications system was once very simple, so simple in fact that an American sailor was able to walk off his ship with cryptographic equipment and sell it to the Soviet Union not just once, but for nearly *twenty years*. When he was finally caught in the mid-'80s, he quipped that Kmart had better security than the US Navy.

The Navy learned its lesson and created a system which, true to its reputation, would become my most pernicious enemy during my time as the *Carney's* communications officer. Indeed, I was more than puzzled when I was told one of the ship's most sensitive responsibilities would be managed by a first tour division officer with absolutely no training in cryptography. Amazingly, this is the norm throughout the Navy.

The electronic key management system, as it was known, lived inside a cramped vault on the ship's main deck. It was the most claustrophobic place on the ship, with only enough room for a single person to sit at a desk hemmed in by safes and bizarre key-breaking equipment. The system at the time used a nearly twenty-year-old operating system that looked more like the menu screen of the original *Oregon Trail* than sophisticated military technology. My job would not be, thankfully, to break codes, but to maintain an inventory of thousands of electronic keys and devices. This, I thought, was not why I joined the Navy. I had visions of driving ships, loading torpedo shells, and shooting big guns, not verifying serial numbers inside a steel closet.

Meanwhile, the wardroom tried to ease me as best they could into the Navy way of doing things. Our days started with "khaki call," a daily meeting of officers and chiefs which, in the Navy, takes its name from the color of our service uniforms. Khaki call was nearly incomprehensible to me during my first few weeks, an exercise in deciphering the daunting world of Navy language and acronyms. It was run by the executive officer, the second-highest-ranking officer on a ship and the captain's right-hand man. While the captain concerned himself primarily with the overall readiness of the ship and her crew, the executive officer, or XO, handled details like the cleanliness of our berthings and day-to-day discipline on board.

Khaki call turned into the perfect opportunity for my boss, Lieutenant Masker, to dole out incomprehensible tasks to me. Since he wasn't in the habit of saying anything a second time, I usually turned to my fellow division officers and, with that desperate shrug known as the "ensign salute," asked for their help. In port, our time not taken up by bridge watch, I had to piece together on my own exactly what the job of a division officer was. The first time I brought Lieutenant Masker a report he had asked for, he gave it a brief glance and replied, "If you're going to hand me a pile of shit, at least double bag it first, and then hand it to me."

Working on a ship, I quickly learned, was not like working in an office.

As junior officers, we rarely stayed in one place and waged a constant battle for access to a desk to actually do our jobs. Though we were higher in rank than many, ensigns were in fact almost dead last in the pecking order of who had earned the right to the ship's short supply of computers. As such, it was notoriously difficult to find anyone during the workday unless they were lucky enough to have a radio. We also had few places to hide as officers; our rank was too conspicuous, and any unqualified ensign caught lounging in the wardroom during the workday by the executive officer or captain would surely have to answer why they weren't dutifully employed. It was especially important on the ship, I realized, to *appear* busy when the right people were looking. We often joked that we could simply walk laps around the ship all day with a folder in one hand and a radio in the other to earn a reputation as a hard worker.

So I spent a lot of time in the radio room getting to know the ITs and their world. One benefit of working in the communications division was that ITs generally stayed in the same place, as most of their equipment and duties lay in radio. Like most young military officers, this was my first real leadership position, so I knew it would take some time before I learned my sailors' job and, more importantly, earned their trust. Before I entered the Navy a family friend and retired commander gave me three important pieces of advice: "Know your job, trust your chief, and lead from the front." I intended to do just that.

Though they were among the hardest-working individuals on the *Carney's* crew, the ITs weren't exactly regarded as her most military-like sailors. They were notorious, rather, for always appearing like they were *not* working. The *Carney's* ITs relished in that reputation and in surprising their superiors when it turned out they knew what they were talking about and had actually done their job. It was a common complaint of the captain that he didn't see enough of my sailors, that they rarely strayed from their nest or showed their face among the crew. Radio garnered a reputation not unlike a high school's AV club, and the ITs only engendered that reputation by treating any stranger who stepped inside with a good amount of suspicion. It didn't help that they also harbored an inherent dislike for the Surface Navy's intense hierarchy.

The ITs were a peculiar group to oversee as an ensign. For one it seemed they had skipped the part of basic training about military bearing. The first impression one got of the *Carney's* radio room was the duty IT, a continuous watch station that monitored naval messages and the status of the ship's radios and networks. The ITs had long maintained a mangled yet surprisingly comfortable office chair for the duty IT to recline in; covered in leopard print patches, with large chunks missing from the armrests, it miraculously held together and served as a bed for the watch stander at night. In the mornings, I would enter radio and often stumble on one of my sailors fully reclined in this chair, covered from head to foot in blankets and snoring unabashedly as incoming message traffic sat unattended on their screen.

Of all the things I had been taught in my short Navy career, surely one of them was that sailors should take their watch station seriously, so I attempted, in those first few days on the *Carney*, to motivate them to put away their blankets and get on with their workday. They sometimes mumbled a "Yes sir," or sometimes nothing at all, as they awoke from their slumber and regretted that a new division officer had entered their midst. (Our captain got the last word—he stumbled on the ITs' Frankenstein chair during a routine inspection of the radio room and ordered me to make it disappear. It was, to the ITs' dismay, replaced with a much less comfortable, government-issued alternative.)

The radio room served as a kind of private sanctuary for the ITs. Locked at all times for the classified information contained inside, the ITs could be sure they would rarely be surprised by unannounced visitors. Lieutenant Masker was the only exception, as he would, on occasion, silently glide into radio for an unofficial inspection. During one of these visits, he discovered one of the ITs' secret stash of protein supplements under the deck plates which, though Masker did not find amusing, had the rest of the division in tears by the time he left. ("I accidentally had these shipped to the ship's address instead of my place.")

The brunt of my work as communications officer was to manage all the equipment in the division and track what needed repair. This was crucial for a ship that would soon deploy and conduct real operations, where everything depended on her ability to communicate and every watch stander would rely on radio circuits and the Internet. During my first months on board, if I wasn't standing watch, I spent as much time as I could getting to know my sailors and the equipment they worked on. I also learned that that equipment, like many things on board a Navy ship, broke a lot.

Though I was, by virtue of my rank, in charge of the communications division, I shared that burden with the ship's chief information systems technician. "Chiefs" comprise the highest enlisted ranks in the Navy and are considered its technical experts. Nearly all division officers lead alongside chiefs, the Navy's "deck plate leaders" who, while the officers sit in their meetings, directly supervise the ship and her sailors. Chiefs dine and socialize in their own mess and only among themselves on a ship, in the same way that officers eat in their own wardrooms. They keep their traditions and ceremonies closely guarded—the chiefs' mess is off-limits even to officers.

Any captain of a ship, then, knows well to listen to his chiefs and to never go over their heads, at least not when the crew is concerned. It is customary, for example, for chiefs to take part in the disciplinary process before the captain if a sailor gets in trouble, or to discuss any proposal about the day-to-day operation of the ship before the captain makes a final decision. At best, the exalted position of the chiefs on a Navy ship can act as an important buffer between officers and enlisted, as they are crucial advisors on how decisions affect sailors' welfare. At its worst, the chiefs' mess devolves into a boys' club (chiefs are overwhelmingly male in the Navy) where their status prevents non-chiefs from holding them accountable for their job. That can also be true, however, of officers.

Chiefs also have the added responsibility of training their first tour officers ("Chiefs train divos" is a common refrain on warships). They are the subject matter experts; we, on the other hand, generally know very little when we arrive on our first ships and take the helm of a division. This somewhat haphazard system doesn't always work as intended because Navy chiefs have varying levels of patience for fresh-faced ensigns. Some take us under their wing and relish the opportunity for mentorship. Others keep us as far away as possible. Luckily, my first chief on the Carney fell in the former category.

A twenty-year-plus veteran of the "Green Gear Navy," comms

technicians who work with land-based units rather than on ships, Senior Chief Petty Officer Theroux was a "chief's chief": boisterous, affable, and supremely dedicated to his sailors. He had a habit of working especially long hours, and when I was ready to go home at the end of the workday, I would often see him at his desk (he was the only one in the division with his own desk), typing furiously at his keyboard and awash in paperwork. As the chief overseeing the entire combat systems department in addition to our division, he focused much of his energy on sorting away his sailors' many administrative needs: their evaluations, awards, qualifications, and personal records. Theroux finished his tour on the *Carney* during her most unforgiving year: deployment workups, a homeport shift to Spain, and her first patrol in the Mediterranean. Like many sailors his family was not with him during this time; he missed the birth of his son while we were somewhere off the coast of Florida. This is not uncommon in the Navy.

Though Theroux was an excellent chief, he was by far not the best technician in the division. His lack of career shipboard experience, and the resulting unfamiliarity with the *Carney's* particular communications suite, meant he couldn't provide the professional expertise his young sailors often needed. Although no one doubted he would always put his sailors first, the other ITs had little trust in his ability to fix anything on board or to advise them on how to do it. That burden instead usually fell to the first class petty officers, or "first classes," as they are called, intermediaries between chiefs and the junior sailors who act as both technicians and mid-level managers. Among the ITs this role was shared by the unfailingly entertaining pair of Petty Officer Tep and Petty Officer Mills.

Mills was the largest sailor on the *Carney*, indeed the largest sailor I ever saw in the Navy, and it was mystifying to all of us how he managed to pass the yearly physical readiness test. On one occasion I witnessed him consume an entire roast chicken for lunch in radio and then proceed directly to a ham sandwich. Though not the most energetic of sailors, Mills was well-liked among the other ITs and could always be trusted to head off confrontations and keep his division focused. His counterpart, Petty Officer Tep, was by far our most expert information systems technician and one of those rare sailors whose personal know-how defied the lackluster formal Navy training he had received. Tep was a pure workhorse; when a problem arose he would attack it furiously until it was resolved. On several occasions on deployment, I saw him hunched over computers and server racks for entire days and nights. "I haven't left radio in the last twenty-four hours even to take a shit!" he once told me. I don't think he was kidding. Though our ship's network never failed to break in entirely unexpected ways, Tep himself never failed to conjure up a solution. I often wondered how we would have survived patrols in the Mediterranean had he not been on board.

It was unfortunate, then, that Tep and Mills were not well-liked by our chain of command. They were, admittedly, not very military-like in appearance and behavior. Both fun-loving by nature, they were not the kind to jump to attention when the captain walked by or to try especially hard to impress their leadership. Appearance is everything in the Navy, and despite their obvious abilities, they didn't exactly fit the mold that many chiefs and officers expected. During one of his evaluations, our captain complained to me about Tep's tattered uniforms and habitual cigarette breaks ("Go to the smoke deck at any time and half of the sailors there will be ITs," he added). Tep also reveled in doing outlandish things like telling officers he wanted to jump on their back and ride them like a monkey or sitting cross-legged on the floor in the combat information center, the ship's tactical watch station, to speak with our department head.

With nearly fifteen years of Navy service to his name, Tep had been passed over for promotion to chief several times. Although his technical grasp of the job far exceeded that of his superiors, his antics had not garnered him an exemplary reputation aboard the *Carney*. As the rest of the chiefs, who rate the first class petty officers on yearly evaluations, saw it, he simply wasn't "chief material" enough to join their ranks. With his unquestionable talents, Tep felt that the ship's leadership had painted an unfair target on his back. Mills, meanwhile, didn't seem particularly concerned with promotion—he waited out his tour on the *Carney* and for his inevitable next tour at a shore command.

There were about ten other sailors in the communications division at any one time on the *Carney*, and they all answered to the first class petty officers and, ultimately, to their chief and to me. Like anywhere in the military, they came from every corner of the country but together composed a hardworking, tight-knit group that didn't let anybody disrespect their hallowed radio room.

Unfortunately, Lieutenant Masker harbored a particular dislike of the ITs. As communications touched everything we did as a ship, and it was the ITs' responsibility to keep radio circuits and the Internet working, their job was especially impactful on board. Masker placed much of his frustration as the man in charge of the ship's technicians on the ITs, whom he always assumed weren't telling the whole truth or hiding things from him. "Don't let your guys blow smoke up your ass," he advised me early on, "and make sure your chief knows his job." As a first tour division officer that put me in a tough position: an uneasy arbiter between my sailors, who didn't like anyone questioning their expertise, and my boss, who didn't like anyone questioning him at all.

Early on during my tour on the *Carney*, as Lieutenant Masker struggled to get his brand-new ensign to understand how to do his job, he advised me to read *A Message to Garcia*, a short essay famous in military circles. It tells the semi-true story of an American named Rowan who, during the Spanish-American War, is entrusted by the president with bringing a letter to "Garcia," an insurgent leader hidden deep within the mountains of Cuba. Rowan takes the letter without a word, disappears into the jungle, and reemerges on the other side of the island three weeks later, his task accomplished. The account occupies a single paragraph, but for the next few pages the author extols the parable of Rowan as an analogy for hard work, determination, and the good old-fashioned American can-do attitude. "Carrying a message to Garcia" implies the ability of seeing a task to its end on one's own and without complaint. "Enterprising men," the essay explains, are often stunted by "the imbecility of the average man— the inability or unwillingness to concentrate on a thing and do it."

A Message to Garcia was written in 1899 yet is still shared today by naval officers as a guide to leadership and military virtue. Masker was using this thinly veiled analogy to motivate me and to get me to motivate the ITs, who more than anybody did not feel the urgency of carrying any message to anybody. Like Rowan, and all the other ensigns on board the ship, I took his advice, kept my head down, and carried the proverbial messages to Garcia. During my two-year tour on the *Carney*, I would come to realize that *A Message to Garcia* had less to say about leadership than about the particular culture of surface warfare officers, and that it was, in truth, a poor substitute for learning to actually motivate your sailors.

Captain Pinckney, in command of the USS *Carney*, himself subscribed unabashedly to this brand of leadership. Pinckney had been in the Navy longer than most of the crew had been alive and was not the kind of leader to inquire into his officers' personal feelings or opinions. He concerned himself with the state of his ship and its mission—the rest was secondary. Though generally pleasant with enlisted sailors, Pinckney was especially hard on his wardroom. If officers gave the wrong answer or presented him with imperfect paperwork, he would offer no leeway for those of us who were new to the ship or to the Navy. During my early days on board, I was sent out of his cabin on more than one occasion with a harsh word about why I didn't know what was going on in the communications division or why the report I had just handed him was so entirely screwed up.

On the one hand, this was the necessary kick in the ass us young ensigns needed to take our job seriously. Inattention to detail, it was quickly explained to us, got sailors hurt, or worse. On the other, it made it that much harder to prepare ourselves for the upcoming deployment. Our captain was clearly not the man to come to with questions or ill-formed ideas. Pinckney, aside from his views on leadership, was one of the moodiest individuals I had ever met. Though he sometimes surprised us with an amusing anecdote, he usually met officers' inquiries with either disdain, frustration, or outright fury. In fact, Pinckney was the only person on the *Carney* who could intimidate Lieutenant Masker, despite my department head's own imposing demeanor. This was made more unsettling by the fact that Pinckney barely stood five and a half feet tall.

In the two months I spent in Mayport leading up to the *Carney's* transatlantic crossing to Spain, every day seemed to hold a new catastrophe that needed solving. Working on a ship, one of the more senior officers explained, meant "putting out fires" every day. Things broke all the time on a warship, and the time to fix them was always *now*.

I was also introduced to the unwelcome surprise of in-port duty. Even with the *Carney* tied to a pier, every member of her crew took turns living on the ship for twenty-four hours to stand watch and act as the ship's emergency responders. Officers were expected to do their part and stand the dreaded officer of the deck in-port watch. When not at sea, the "officer of the deck" was a glorified security guard: they stood behind a podium on the quarterdeck, the entrance to the ship at the end of the brow, with a gun strapped to their hip for five hours at a time.

Not long after my arrival on the *Carney*, I was quickly assigned to officer of the deck watch. The requisite knowledge to guard a multibillion-dollar warship, it turned out, was relatively minimal: Knowing how to shoot a gun and recognize a few nautical flags got me most of the way there. Any glamour in being entrusted with such a responsibility was quickly brushed aside, as standing for five hours in full uniform and a Kevlar vest in the Florida humidity was as arduous as it sounds. With only one other enlisted sailor as my companion, who wrote in the ship's log and passed words over the general announcing system, I had little to do but salute sailors as they stepped on board and serve as the unofficial messenger boy for just about every member of the crew. At night the watch continued because, like a Wal-Mart, a Navy ship stays open twenty-four hours. If one wants to see true desperation, look no further than the officer of the deck on a deployed ship who, while his friends go merrily ashore to enjoy a night out, must stare vigilantly at a concrete pier in a foreign land.

To make matters worse, the qualification course for officer of the deck required being pepper sprayed. By itself this would be painful enough, but we were also forced to endure a ridiculous obstacle course to prove one's mettle as a Navy watch stander. Immediately after getting pepper spray shot into my face at point-blank range, an experience not unlike having your eyes doused in gasoline and lit on fire, I spent nearly five minutes swinging a foam baton at a sailor dressed in a padded suit who was doing his best to knock me to the ground. In addition to the embarrassment from the massive amount of snot streaming from my nose, I failed to land a single blow on the "red man," as he was dubbed for the color of his pads. When the ship's master at arms deemed I had had enough, I stumbled to the open water hose a fellow junior officer was mercifully holding for me. The best part of being pepper sprayed still lay ahead; however, as it turned out the powerful solution didn't wash off your face even after holding your head under a hose for ten minutes. Later that day the burning feeling returned with a vengeance, and I quickly retired to the JO Jungle to reflect on my decision to join the Surface Navy.

People respond to pepper spray in wildly different ways. A small number, through a strange genetic disposition, are barely affected by it. Others, and these are by far the most fun to watch, simply fall to their ground, assume the fetal position, and break out into uncontrollable screams. I was somewhere in the middle, though regardless of which camp one fell into, in the end no junior officer escaped the burden of quarterdeck watch. It seemed our recruiters had conveniently left out this part of the SWO job description.

Thankfully I was not the new guy for long after my arrival on the *Carney*. Before our departure to Spain, a slew of new ensigns checked in to replace officers whose tours were soon coming to an end. They arrived newly commissioned from the Naval Academy, Navy ROTC, or, like me, Officer Candidate School. Also like me, they were learning the routine and the vocabulary of shipboard life for the first time. Over the next two years, we would undergo the many qualifications required to eventually earn our surface warfare officer pin, and together experience over a year at sea, our fair share of foreign ports, and some truly memorable leadership (for good or bad). For now, though, we were just trying to keep our heads above water.

The JO Jungle was integral to our survival during our first tour, as it was the only place to find privacy and where no department head dared enter. The only time our sanctuary was invaded was during the executive officer's occasional berthing inspections, during which he decried our home's lack of cleanliness and general unmilitary-like appearance. More than once on deployment we heard the announcement "*Assemble all berthing five occupants in berthing five*" over the ship's loudspeaker system and, upon arriving, received a lecture from the XO about setting the example for the rest of the ship. But no matter how many times he admonished us, the Jungle always returned to its old ways.

SWOs have earned a reputation in the Navy for being eager to stab each other in the back to get ahead in their wardroom. As the *Carney's* most junior officers, we vowed we would never fall to the cutthroat mentality known as the "SWO dagger," the metaphorical weapon with which officers betray their peers. Indeed, the boys of the JO Jungle remained a surprisingly cohesive unit throughout our deployments and never allowed the pressures of life at sea to derail our good cheer. Sure, every once in a while someone would punch a locker or smash the phone against the bulkhead, but for the most part the Jungle remained our private sanctuary.

CHAPTER 3

This Is Some Real Nautical Shit!

The USS *Carney* did not just remain tied to the pier in the months before her departure to Spain. She would start her first Mediterranean patrol soon after arrival and was, while still in Mayport, scheduled for a series of pre-deployment exercises and workups. In late June, I went out to sea for the first time as a surface warfare officer in training.

The morning of our departure, my first time getting underway on a Navy ship, was both exhilarating and terrifying. This was why I joined the Navy in the first place, yet I had been warned by other junior officers of sleepless nights and *Carney's* brutal watch schedule. My only nautical experience up to that point had been in a simulator. How would I fare on the *Carney's* bridge?

As I walked onto the ship's brow in the predawn hours, *Carney* was already a hive of activity. Awaking a sleeping eight-thousand-ton vessel and sailing out of a harbor and into open ocean is a serious operation in the Navy. Deep in the ship's bowels, the engineers made last-minute checks to her four enormous gas turbine engines, her steering system, and the intricate web of machinery that would propel *Carney* through the water. Our navigator and her quartermasters, up on the bridge, reviewed our electronic charts and their plan to get the ship out of Mayport's small basin. Technicians turned on radars and radios, while the cooks in the galley prepared to feed nearly three hundred mouths for the weeks-long voyage.

I would have no role to play in taking *Carney* out to sea. As Lieutenant Masker instructed, my responsibility was to show up on the bridge, disappear in the background, and simply watch. Maneuvering a ship away from a pier is a complex dance, one that would require dozens of people on the ship's bridge to execute. Orchestrating it all was our captain, who calmly sat on his chair (only the captain and the executive officer have the privilege of sitting on the bridge) while reports poured in from his department heads.

When the hour of departure arrived, *Carney* came alive. Her turbines began spinning, her radars rotating, and smoke billowed out of her stacks. In the harbor, a pair of tugboats glided toward the ship and attached themselves to our bow and our stern. Inside the bridge, the officer of the deck, a junior officer with barely more experience than me, requested permission from the captain to take in all lines and get underway. One by one, the six Kevlar ropes that had held *Carney* to her pier for months were thrown into the water and pulled onto her decks.

Once free, the tugboats pulled the ship into the basin and her two powerful propellers began spinning furiously. After a few seconds, the enormous warship slowly moved forward and the captain ordered her bow pointed at the harbor's exit. Mayport's small basin is separated from the ocean by a simple rock wall, or breakwater, and in a few minutes *Carney* quickly found herself in the Atlantic. Meanwhile, along with the other new ensigns, I was doing my best to stay out of people's way.

Once in open ocean, the eight-thousand-ton destroyer began to pitch and roll with the swell. For the first time in my Navy career I experienced the uneasy feeling, and the pounding headache, that accompanied being out to sea. The human body, it turned out, did not appreciate leaving terra firma. Unfortunately a warship has no patience for sailors' personal discomforts, and I quickly learned that work on a warship only intensified at sea. *Carney's* complex system of machinery and electronics now required continual attention. On the bridge, the officers began the ceaseless rotation of watches that would keep the ship on course and safely away from other vessels. In fact, only a few minutes after leaving Mayport, I was given the unwelcome news that I was to stand the "mid-watch" that very night, from 10 p.m. to 2 a.m.

If I felt out of place aboard *Carney* on land, I was even more "lost in the sauce" at sea. The officers who had already tasted life underway fell unconsciously back into a rhythm dictated by their watch schedule. They knew instinctively, for example, that it was ill-advised to forgo sleep before a night watch, or that life at sea no longer meant nights of uninterrupted sleep. Instead, sailors rested whenever they could, particularly officers whose watch schedules were entirely sporadic. As an ambitious ensign, of course, I confidently stayed awake until my first ever Navy watch.

At night, *Carney's* bridge was nearly pitch-black so that our eyes could adjust to the darkness and make out other vessels' lights on the horizon. When I climbed the long ladder well to the bridge that night, I was astonished that anyone could navigate a ship in such conditions. I immediately bumped into other watch standers and equipment and was so disoriented I could barely find the officer of the deck, who I'd be reporting to during my watch. Outside, I could not tell where the sea ended and the sky began. It would take me a few weeks before I memorized the layout of the bridge and could navigate it with confidence. For now, I relied only on the dim glow of its instrument panels to guide my way around.

Standing watch at night is something no mariner ever truly gets comfortable with, and that's a good thing. Nearly every SWO I've known, myself included, has had close calls on night watches with barely lit sailboats and tiny fishing vessels, sometimes in traffic lanes where all one could see was the red, green, and white lights marking thirty-thousand-ton cargo ships. After my first two night watches in a row, I questioned how I would maintain that rhythm on a months-long deployment.

Life out to sea took on a new routine. Well into our first deployment we stood watch in a three-section rotation, a system known as "five and dime" in the Navy, in which we stood continuous five-hour watches followed by ten hours off. These ten hours, however, were not left to ourselves.

Our role as division officers continued at sea, and the time not on watch was spent managing our sailors, overseeing our equipment, and taking orders from our department heads. The requisite meetings (and SWOs *love* meetings) also did not stop; we held khaki meetings, officer meetings, planning meetings for training, planning meetings for maintenance, training sessions, daily operations briefs, briefs for navigational transits, briefs for flight operations, and briefs for every other conceivable Navy evolution. When I wasn't sitting in a meeting or learning my job in radio, I began the mountain of qualifications required to earn my surface warfare qualification. If there was time left in the day, I sometimes managed to sleep.

New as I was to my division, watch on the bridge became the focus of my attention in those first weeks underway. The *Carney's* bridge was *our* domain as officers. The ITs had their radio, the engineers had their plant, but on the bridge is where we felt at home. While enlisted sailors requested permission to enter the bridge, officers came and went as they pleased. Though in port we acted more like administrators and managers than warfighters, when the ship was out to sea none of our responsibilities held more weight than standing watch.

Carney was twenty years old by the time I arrived, and her age was starting to show. If you want to see the latest navigational technology, go aboard pleasure yachts and cruise ships, not Navy warships. Her bridge, except for the addition of GPS and electronic charts, was not much different from the Navy of our grandparents. We drove her the same way too, with an officer calling out orders to a helmsman, who physically turned the wheel and operated the engine's throttles.

The *Carney's* bridge team was a mix of officers and enlisted sailors. The helm was generally manned by the ship's most junior sailors, with oversight from a more senior boatswain's mate. There was also a quartermaster, a navigation specialist who assisted the officers in managing the ship's chart and official logs.

The officers managed this small team and navigated the ship. The conning officer, or "conn," kept their eyes out at sea and passed rudder and engine orders to the helmsman. This was the first underway watch new surface officers stood and thus did so under the careful eye of the officer of the deck, or OOD, who was overall charged with the safe navigation of the ship. As the direct representative of the captain, who could not spend all his time on the bridge, this was one of the most important watch stations on board and the ultimate qualification an officer earned during their first tour. A third officer, the junior officer of the deck, assisted the OOD in navigating the ship and in carrying out the ship's daily routine.

With a second tour division officer as my OOD and mentor, I alternated between conning officer and junior officer of the deck and got a crash course in the craft of navigation, or at least the Navy version of it. I mastered maneuvering and speed commands and how a huge steel vessel responded to the turn of her rudders. I learned how to read an electronic chart and keep a ship on course. I trained myself to continually monitor the weather: the wind's direction and speed, the barometric pressure, and where clouds were forming in the sky. I became familiar with the mariner's essential equipment: radars, compasses, and one's eyes. Indeed, the most important skill I learned as a mariner was how to look out a window, because knowing what to look for on the ocean wasn't as obvious as it seemed. We looked for other vessels, especially small ones that didn't appear clearly on a radar. We looked for changes in the weather, for ripples or whitecaps on the water that signaled wind, or clouds approaching in the distance. We scanned for whales or trash on the ocean surface. We looked for anything out of the ordinary, anything that stood out against the vast monotonous blue.

The other thing I learned about standing watch on the bridge was that it was relentlessly boring. Most of the time nothing happened out to sea. Except for those rare moments when we transited congested channels and straits, we were surrounded by only water and saw only a handful of other ships during a five-hour watch. Electronic charts and GPS, to be sure, have made navigation and ship-driving deceivingly simple. Only a few decades ago mariners out of sight of land could only determine their position by measuring angles to stars and planets and plotting their course and speed by hand on a paper chart. On the *Carney* it only took a quick glance at a computer screen to find out exactly where we were. Deployed in the Mediterranean, I would come to have my fair share of terrifying watches on the bridge and, in turn, garner a deep respect for the responsibility we held as surface warfare officers. For now, however, as we idled off the coast of northern Florida, our only real concern was the frequent, driving rains and the fog banks so intense that we could barely see our own bow from the bridge.

Before returning to Mayport during our few weeks at sea, we conducted a towing exercise with USS *The Sullivans*, another *Arleigh Burke*-class destroyer. Though part of our pre-deployment training, Navy ships don't generally tow anything, that's what tugboats are for, so the captain and the officers involved expressed some amount of hesitation about our crew's lack of preparedness. Like everything in the Navy, even a towing evolution came with a five-hundred-page manual, though it was doubtful anyone on board had actually read it. Because I had no role on the bridge for the exercise, I observed it on the forecastle (pronounced "foc'sle"), the forward part of the upper deck, with some of the other ensigns and safely behind the forward-mounted gun.

Carney was acting as the towed ship and *The Sullivans* as the ship towing. While we maintained a slow, steady course, *The Sullivans* closed in on us from astern and drifted past our ship at what, for a warship, was uncomfortably close, about one hundred yards. At that distance, one false turn of the rudder and both our nearly two-billion-dollar destroyers could have collided. Sailors on *The Sullivans*, using a specialized rifle, shot a long, thin line attached to the actual towing cable onto our forecastle. Because of the length of this first line, our boatswain's mates could heave it in and have enough time to secure the towing line to a series of bitts and the hawsehole at the very nose of our ship, all this before *The Sullivans* could sail too far past us and take her towing line along with her.

But as the boatswain's mate handling the line that day, Petty Officer Wiler, began twisting the line around bitts on the forecastle, he realized *The Sullivans* was moving too fast alongside the *Carney* to give our sailors enough time to heave in the cable and secure it to the nose of our ship. Wiler was a boatswain's mate, sailors who work topside and do the more "sailor-like" things on board like moor the ship, drive the small boat, and man the wheel on the bridge. As any self-respecting boatswain's mate would, Wiler refused to let go of the line and instead continued to grasp it with both hands as *The Sullivans* continued to edge ahead of *Carney's* nose. He was, essentially, single-handedly attempting to hold back an eight-thousand-ton warship.

Eventually the line, under the enormous tension of that warship, snapped out of Wiler's hands and whipped through the bitts it had been wrapped around behind him. As it completely unwound, the metal clasp at the end of the line flew off the bitts and smacked Wiler almost directly in the crotch. He fell to the ground and we heard a loud scraping noise as the towing cable dragged along our forecastle and fell into the water in front of the ship. Our chief corpsman, the Navy word for a medic, was already on the forecastle and rushed to Wiler's side. He tore open his coveralls and, exposing Wiler to everyone assembled on the forecastle and the watch standers on the bridge above, saw that the metal clasp had struck him in the inner thigh. Wiler was back on his feet by the end of the day, and with *The Sullivans* now a safe distance from *Carney*, we didn't attempt the exercise again. The crew did, however, gain an infamous anecdote that day: the tale of how Petty Officer Wiler almost lost his balls because he thought he could hold back a destroyer.

The incident was a lesson to us newbies that ships were dangerous places and that sailors put their lives in officers' hands when we stood watch on the bridge. Just a few days later, in fact, *The Sullivans* attempted to fire an SM-2 missile from her forward deck during another exercise. It misfired and broke apart above the forecastle immediately after launch. Thankfully no sailors were hurt.

The *Carney*, meanwhile, completed her pre-deployment exercises and certifications. Gunner's mates shot their heavy machine guns at fake targets, fire controlmen practiced Tomahawk missile and antiballistic missile launch scenarios, engineers prepared their entire plant for inspection, and officers practiced drills and precision anchorages from the bridge. For much of this I was, as Lieutenant Masker often liked to remind me, "lost in the sauce." I observed as many of these events as I could, though participated in very few, and tried to soak up as much as I could through the proverbial "firehose" of information. Among the ensigns, we began to realize that the SWO community was living up to its reputation; it was clear there was no formal system in place to train surface officers in much of anything. It amounted to handing us a binder of qualifications, each with hundreds of items to observe, and wishing us good luck.

My new boss wasn't much help either. Masker had no interest in my qualifications; to him they were something for me to get out of the way as quickly as I could every day so I could focus on my job as commo. Masker also had a peculiar habit of climbing up to the bridge during quiet moments at night to sneak up on the officers on watch. He would quietly insert himself between watch standers and simply wait until someone noticed him which, because the pilothouse remained entirely darkened at night, often took some time. On several occasions while standing watch, my eyes fixed out the windows as conning officer or junior officer of the deck, I was startled by a dark form standing absolutely still beside me, one much larger than I knew the rest of my watch team members to be. It was Masker, who, upon being noticed, wryly remarked something like "Everything good up here?" The reason for these visitations remained a mystery. Was he evaluating my performance on the bridge? Was this part of his sardonic sense of humor? Or was he just bored and in need of some fresh air topside? If anything, it added to his notorious reputation as the wardroom's boogeyman. Indeed, every officer, even the ones who didn't work for him, were on constant alert for Masker as they made their way through the ship's passageways.

Carney returned to her pier inside Mayport's basin in early August, her crew hardened by its time at sea and ready for deployment. For now, we enjoyed our last month stateside before the transit to Spain. It was hurricane season in Florida, and all ships on base were on alert to sortie out to sea if a storm came through. This nearly occurred with Tropical Storm Erika, though it dissipated before touching Mayport. "This is why I tried to get stationed in San Diego," a boatswain's mate explained to me one night on quarterdeck watch. "Fucking Florida ..."

In September the USS *Carney* left Mayport for good. She made a short stop at a Navy weapons station in Yorktown, Virginia, to onload her deployment complement of missiles and ammunition, then sailed east. Eleven days later, after a quiet transit across the Atlantic, *Carney* moored at Naval Base Rota in Spain. Located just west of the Strait of Gibraltar, the waterway that separates the Atlantic Ocean from the Mediterranean Sea and Europe from Africa, Rota is a quiet Spanish village lined with cobblestone streets, a sprawling beach, and striking Medieval architecture. Its naval base still belongs to the Spanish but the American military has maintained a presence there since the 1950s. That's not surprising given its geographical importance to the US Navy—all ships must traverse the Strait of Gibraltar on their way to the Mediterranean.

In Rota, many of *Carney's* sailors and their families were living abroad for the first time. The Spanish, though among the friendlier people on the continent, did not generally speak English, and Rota's economy still catered mainly to the influx of Spanish tourists that swarmed the town in summer. Left to figure out Spanish menus and road signs on their own, many of the Americans working at Naval Base Rota did not venture very often into town and got much of their needs from the base's American-style department store. For our part, the JO Jungle did its best to take in the local culture. We ate in small restaurants and learned that the Spaniards love potatoes, cured ham, and tiny fried fish. We ventured into the region's stunning countryside. Some of us even attempted to talk to Spanish women. It usually did not go well.

Sadly, work on the ship didn't stop for us to enjoy our European vacation. The days only got busier, in fact, as we prepared to leave for deployment only a month after our arrival in Rota. Lieutenant Masker's mood, meanwhile, worsened as we neared our departure date. Along with the other department heads, the pressure mounted from a captain whose tour as commanding officer seemed to rest entirely on *Carney's* first patrol as a Rota destroyer. "Shit rolls downhill" in the Navy, meaning if the captain was angry at his department heads because things on the ship were breaking, you could bet *they* would in turn take it out on their division officers, especially the young first tour ensigns who had yet to learn the subtle SWO art of standing up to your department head.

Because of the indispensable role communications would play for a deployed ship, from her UHF radios to her computer network, it was especially critical that the radio room, and her sailors, be in working order. The only time Masker betrayed his normally icy demeanor was during a morning khaki call when I couldn't explain why one of our servers was entirely down. I hadn't been aware, in fact, that something was wrong in the first place. Masker abruptly ended our huddle of departmental managers, before Senior Chief Theroux had a chance to come to my rescue: "Delloue, why don't you go down to radio and figure this out and then come back and tell me why you don't know what the fuck is going on in your division." I learned at that moment that when your shit is broken in the Navy, you better find out before your boss does.

In truth, I was probably among the more fortunate of the ensigns. At least I wasn't in the engineering department. Aboard Navy ships there exists an unquestionable distinction between engineers and those the engineers call "topsiders," that is, anyone who is not an engineer. Despite their moniker as the ship's "grease monkeys," the *Carney's* engineering rates were among the toughest on board. While some of us enjoyed the ocean's gentle breeze on our faces on watch, these sailors toiled in the ship's bilges and maintained her engines, her oil pumps, her electrical switchboards, and even her sewage pipes. Their coveralls often coated in oil and marine fuel, engineers had the dirtiest jobs, consistently worked the longest days, and got the least share of the glory. "I used to work in a mine back in Tennessee," one of the hull maintenance technicians, who worked on piping, once told me. "This job isn't much different." Sailors who felt they had gotten the short end of the stick when it came to their job (perhaps they had been convinced by their recruiter that being a machinist's mate wouldn't be so bad) were often reminded by their shipmates of a quintessential Navy maxim: "Choose your rate, choose your fate." This wasn't much in the way of solace, but in the Navy, if your life sucks, *get used to it.*

As officers, those on the ship who were in the *least* danger of getting dirty, engineering was the last place we wanted to work in. For one, the *Carney* suffered from a string of particularly strange and incompetent chief engineers, the officers in charge of the engineering department. One was so aloof we surmised he was an alien in a human suit, like the guy in *Men in Black* who only drinks sugar water. Masker may have been hard on me, but at least he wasn't a fool. In a twenty-year-old ship, being an engineering officer also meant your job was the wardroom's most unpredictable and time-consuming. Machinery broke often and always in the most inopportune times, and, though officers themselves certainly weren't turning any wrenches, if the engineers stayed late to fix something it was expected that their division officer would too.

The primary duty of engineering officers was, in practice, to write casualty reports for broken equipment and send these out as naval messages. It didn't matter if the ship was underway and they had watch at 2 a.m. that night; if it was 10 p.m. and some piece of equipment shit the bed, they could forget about seeing their rack. This was a peculiar policy considering we were the ones driving the ship when on watch and, more than our department heads, needed the rest, though it wasn't something our leadership took the least notice of. When the phone rang in the middle of the night in the JO Jungle, it was likely to be the chief engineer looking for his auxiliaries or propulsion officer. The "fuck you" SWO attitude came down especially hard on those ensigns who worked in the engineering department.

CHAPTER 4
Underway. Shift Colors.

In early November, a little after a month after her arrival in Spain, the USS *Carney* and her crew of three hundred sailors went out to sea once more for her first four-month patrol in the Mediterranean Sea. On the transit out I was assigned as conning officer, my first opportunity to drive the ship during a major evolution. While driving in open ocean is relatively straightforward, conning a ship either on or off a pier is a more complex operation and requires a considerable amount of experience and skill. In the Navy, this kind of "ship handling," as it is known, is conducted with a substantial addition of watch standers to the bridge. Because of the lack of formal seamanship training for officers, there is no distinction between being qualified to drive ships out to sea and being qualified to handle them inside a harbor. Young junior officers are considered capable of driving eight-thousand-ton warships away from a concrete pier, then, with a little practice in a simulator and almost no real-life experience.

Yet, though I was qualified on paper, in practice it was always the commanding officer who drove the ship in close-quarters situations on the *Carney*. No captain in the Navy, in fact, would have risked his ship in the hands of a first tour ensign, regardless of whether they trained for twelve weeks at Officer Candidate School or four years at the Naval Academy. Even academy graduates, surprisingly, lacked the formal training to reliably drive warships off a pier when they first reported to their ship. Conning officers during such evolutions, then, acted more like parrots: They relayed the orders of the captain to the helmsmen standing behind the wheel and engine throttles inside the pilothouse. More than anything, such opportunities were a way for Pinckney to observe his new officers under pressure and test them through the noise and chaos of the bridge.

My first test didn't exactly go well, though I would soon learn it was hard for anything to go well in the hands of Captain Pinckney. Leaving Rota, like Mayport, was a straightforward affair. There was no channel to navigate, and once a ship left the tight exit of the breakwater she had only to find the buoy marking safe water and sail in its general direction. Even inside the breakwater, there was plenty of space to maneuver the ship and get her nose pointed in the right direction. Although every ship handling evolution came with a certain amount of risk, Naval Base Rota was not an especially difficult example. But this was Pinckney's first time leaving for deployment as captain, and before we had even pulled our lines in, his emotions bubbled to the surface.

Pinckney and I stood together on the bridgewing, looking down at the pier while the two helmsmen responded to our orders inside the bridge. Inside the basin, two powerful tugboats were attached to our stern and bow and would help pull *Carney* away from the pier. The captain began issuing rudder and engine orders, which I then passed on to the helmsmen: "Right standard rudder ... starboard engine back one-third ... port engine ahead one-third." When "handling" a ship, or maneuvering it in close quarters to a pier or other ships, a conning officer balances the ahead and astern forces of the ship's engines to stay in place and use the rudder to push the ship's stern away from the pier. After sailors on the main deck had pulled all mooring lines onto the ship, and nothing remained to connect us to the pier, the boatswain's mate of the watch blew his whistle and announced over the speaker system: "Underway. Shift colors." Slowly, the *Carney's* enormous frame began to glide away from the pier. A civilian harbor pilot, a standard feature when maneuvering Navy ships inside a harbor, stood close to us and issued directions to the tugboats via radio.

A ship on the water acts like a giant seesaw: Apply force at her stern with her engines and her bow will swing in the opposite direction, and vice versa. This is where ship handling turns into somewhat of an art form: It takes enormous concentration and expertise to balance engines and tugs to "lift" a ship evenly away from a pier. If a ship does not pivot correctly, with both ends leaving the pier at the same time, the bow or stern can easily smash into the concrete wall one is trying to get away from. There is hardly a SWO who hasn't experienced this in the simulator and not been, thereafter, traumatized that it would happen to them in real life. It was also exactly what started to happen as we attempted to pull *Carney* into the Rota basin for the first time.

Pinckney, seeing the stern starting to move back toward the pier as the bow was being pulled too hard by the forward tug, switched into panic mode and furiously sputtered out new orders: "Right full rudder! Port and starboard engine ahead two-thirds!" I relayed his orders as swiftly as I could to the helmsmen in the pilothouse. In the rushed attempt to get the stern moving in the right direction, Kenny lost track of our engine configuration. "Where are my engines at?" He balked at me. Unfortunately I was, by that point, experiencing complete tunnel vision; shifting my eyes between the pier and the rudder indicator on the bridgewing, I had also lost track of my last engine order. All I could manage was a confused "Huh?" which was the last response a junior officer should give to his captain on the bridge.

Beating his fists on the bridgewing's wooden panels, Kenny screamed: "WHERE ARE MY FUCKING ENGINES AT?!" I stammered my best guess: "All engines ahead two-thirds!" By then, because engine orders always take some time to have effect on a ship, our stern was already lifting off the pier and *Carney* righted herself. Kenny was incensed; "Pay attention, goddamnit!" Around us the bridge had gone dead calm. Finally away from danger, and our nose already pointed in the right direction, I ordered a course to the helmsman to leave the harbor. As we left the breakwater we saw Cadiz, one of the oldest cities in Europe, not far off our port side. *Carney* was on deployment.

Kenny's outburst on the bridge left me troubled. This was my first naval evolution, and a rather basic one at that, yet it had been a rather poor performance. I felt like my eyes had glazed over during the entire evolution, like it had all been a blur and I had lost all situational awareness. Among the junior officers, we also began feeling uneasy about the captain's state of mind. Was this what we had to look forward to every time we stepped on the bridge? Maybe I was simply no ship handler. I had the next four months to find out.

Destroyers like the USS *Carney* are designed to protect large, high-value ships like aircraft carriers and amphibious ships. Sometimes, they sail off on their own to conduct independent missions and maintain an American maritime presence in the world's major waterways. Destroyers are enormously versatile; they can hunt submarines, shoot down aircraft, conduct surveillance missions, strike targets on land with artillery fire or Tomahawk missiles, or simply intimidate the hell out of just about anyone. The year *Carney* arrived in Rota marked the start of a renewed American presence in sixth fleet, the Navy's area of operations that includes the Mediterranean Sea and all the waters surrounding Europe. Specifically, the four destroyers now stationed in Spain would rotate in and out of Rota and be charged primarily with protecting Israel and Europe from ballistic missiles, powerful nuclear weapons that could travel into the stratosphere and strike targets thousands of miles away. Ballistic defense ships, or BMD, ships like the *Carney* were equipped with special SM-3 missiles designed to shoot ballistic missiles out of the sky, just as they reached the apex of their trajectory. We would, essentially, be the last line of defense against nuclear-capable countries like Iran and the "little rocket man" who, at the time, occupied our collective imagination.

As we began our first deployment, the Navy's focus in Europe was already shifting from Iran and the Middle East to a more familiar adversary. The civil war in Syria had reached a breaking point, and Russia, from its small naval base in the Syrian town of Tartus, was sending missiles onto the enemies of Bashar al-Assad's government. With a bolstered presence in the Mediterranean Sea, the US Navy decided to use its new Rota destroyers to keep an eye on Russia's renewed ambitions in the region.

In fact, a number of tense interactions occurred around this time between the Russian and US Navies that set the stage for all my deployment on the

Carney. In April of 2014 the USS *Donald Cook*, another of the Rota-based destroyers, was operating in international waters in the Black Sea when a Russian Su-24 fighter jet screamed toward her and flew only feet above her mast. The incident, caught on video from the bridge of the *Donald Cook*, made headlines in the US and caused a good amount of consternation for the commanding officers of the Rota ships. No aircraft, especially not a military aircraft, was supposed to fly that close to a warship.

The *Donald Cook's* captain might well have been justified in shooting down that aircraft, a decision that ultimately rested entirely with him. Do nothing and you could hazard your entire ship, but shoot first, and you could take down an unarmed aircraft and start an international incident. Almost any captain would have opted for the former choice and taken the first hit rather than start World War III. Besides, *Cook* was in Russia's backyard in the Black Sea. So her captain did nothing, and rightly so, because as it turned out that Su-24 didn't have any weapons loaded at the time. Whether or not the Russian Navy meant for that aircraft to fly so close to an American warship, or whether it was the idea of a particularly brazen pilot, we'll never know, but the interaction, among others, left no question that our old Cold War rivalry had been given new life.

After leaving Rota for the first time, however, I wasn't thinking about any of that. I was trying to figure out how to run the communications division and stand watch on the bridge. As a SWO, albeit as yet unqualified, I was learning to juggle the dueling responsibilities of being a mariner and a division officer all at once. As a first tour ensign I had the added burden of not knowing what the hell I was doing on either of those fronts.

Once out to sea we turned right instead of left. This was unexpected. Rota is on the Atlantic side of Spain, so turning right meant we were not going into the Mediterranean but heading north along the Atlantic coast instead. Being the newest ship in sixth fleet, we had been ordered to intercept a newly constructed Russian submarine in the English Channel and follow her to the most likely destination, the coast of Syria and the Russian naval base at Tartus. After leaving Rota, then, we sailed north along the Portuguese coast and crossed the Bay of Biscay all the way to the northwestern arm of France, where we were scheduled to refuel before our assignment further up in the channel. On the way we anchored in the bay near Brest, France, where, coincidentally, my father had been stationed on a French submarine nearly thirty years before.

The *Carney* moored at the port in Cherbourg for only a few hours to refuel. With no time for sailors to leave the ship, we could only look on beyond the pier and hope for croissants another day. Once underway again, we sailed inside the English Channel to wait for the Russian submarine. By then the temperature had plummeted, and as the winter weather settled in, the sea swells increased to thirteen feet, not uncommon in that latitude but powerful enough to rock our ship hard. Since destroyers are relatively narrow to maximize speed through the water and are top-heavy from the size of their mast, they tend to roll severely from side to side when the sea acts up. Warships are not designed to withstand heavy weather and the Navy's policy is to avoid it altogether. It is common for ships, in fact, to alter their routes or schedule to avoid storms entirely.

In thirteen-foot seas, anything that was not tied down inside the ship, including people, was likely to be thrown across the other side of a space when the ship took a heavy swell or made a sharp turn. Carelessly walking about the ship or up and down ladder wells, without a firm grip on a handrail, was an excellent way to seriously injure oneself. In those conditions, going about one's daily routine on board took on a ridiculous dimension, like having your office fully shaken every few minutes. Seasickness affected nearly everyone, albeit in varying degrees, from a minor inconvenience to utter incapacitation. I found myself somewhat in the middle. On the bridge, seeing the ocean and her movements, and taking in fresh air from the bridgewing, usually cured me of all nausea. It was being inside, though, without portholes to look through and staring at computer screens while the room swayed from side to side, that made work nearly impossible. There were those who couldn't function even on watch and had to carry plastic bags to vomit in. It didn't help that anything you intended to use, if it wasn't secured or tied to something, routinely disappeared behind cabinets or equipment racks. Many coffee mugs were lost that way and, to the joy of their previous owner, stumbled on months later during post-deployment deep cleans.

Thanksgiving came while we idled in the channel and waited for the

Russians. It is up to the captain how a ship celebrates holidays, although it is customary to allow the crew days off from work or "holiday routine" during those times. Holiday routine is derided as "holiday for some, routine for others" in the Navy. On a deployed ship it is impossible to actually get days off, because for almost all sailors work cannot stop on board. They have to keep the engineering plant churning, the radios working, the radars scanning, the weapons ready, and the ship moving. Some watches, like the bridge, are entirely unaffected by holiday routine. We could not relax our readiness in the English Channel because it happened to be Thanksgiving in America. Besides watch, however, we could expect our department heads to ease up on our duties as division officers during those days. For us ensigns, holiday routine, which was also generally granted every Sunday, was a welcome opportunity to study for our qualifications, exercise, or simply get a few extra hours of sleep.

The captain decided during this time to hold a Thanksgiving dinner for the officers in our service khaki uniforms. Since the turnover of watches was scheduled to coincide with mealtimes, it was difficult in the first place to get everyone in the wardroom at the same time. It was expected, nevertheless, that those officers who had an upcoming watch should attend the beginning of the dinner, while those coming off of watch should attend the end. Even those with night watches, who relied on the evening hours to get much-needed sleep, were not exempt. In fact, that first Thanksgiving dinner started a tradition of mandatory attendance at all wardroom events. Such formality in wardroom dynamics is a common feature in the Surface Navy, indeed even among the wardrooms of other nations' navies that I visited while in Europe. On some cruisers, the captains of which are higher ranked than on destroyers, I heard of officers having to stand behind their chairs for every meal until the commanding officer entered the wardroom. At Officer Candidates School, we were required to complete an online tutorial on how to set a table for a formal dinner. This culture finds its roots deep in naval tradition and the Age of Sail, when officers occupied the aft part of the ship, with their own quarters and wardroom, and enlisted sailors strung up hammocks and ate together in the forward part of the ship. Hence the saying, attributed to Horatio Nelson: "*Aft the more honour, forward the better man!*" The formal nature of officer culture persists awkwardly to this day, though in the modern world it mostly appears ridiculous except to officers who have spent too long in the Navy to notice it anymore.

On the evening of the dinner, our cooks set the wardroom table with our finest cutlery and holiday decorations. We arrived on time and stood behind our chairs to await the captain. When he finally arrived and the food was served, the ship began to rock heavily as the seas outside intensified. The wardroom, a few decks above the waterline, swayed violently as the eight-thousand-ton vessel bounced in the swells. With every roll we had to hold not just ourselves in our chairs, which without our gripping the table would crash into the bulkheads, but everything laid out on the table as well. It was a hell of a moment to have brought out every table dressing we owned. Inevitably we could not save everything, so we tried our best to hold pitchers of water and juice first as these were the most likely to cause damage. Forks and knives slid off the table and bread rolls became missile hazards at our feet. In between moments of literally holding the table together, we slipped in bites of food. This was, after all, Thanksgiving dinner. The evening resulted in a lot of soiled uniforms.

The captain took this in his usually poor humor. Every officer was on edge and was painfully aware that his brilliant idea had come to naught. In the Surface Navy it is highly frowned on, in fact forbidden in an unspoken kind of way, to criticize or make light of the captain's decisions. Pinckney's sensitivity to this was notorious; he became especially sullen and withdrawn when he felt he was being ridiculed. At the time no one laughed, not openly so at least, and I felt like the atmosphere in the wardroom could have been cut with a knife (which were all, incidentally, on the floor). Pinckney mostly enjoyed his turkey in silence, while I eagerly awaited my upcoming five-hour watch, which would allow me to leave the wardroom.

By this point in the deployment, I had become somewhat more hardened to bridge watch which, though was by far more enjoyable than the administrative toil of managing a division, was admittedly often dull. As an ensign with little experience, I usually took the watch as the conning officer. In the channel, this involved mostly making turns inside an imaginary box our navigator drew up on our chart; we remained south of the shipping lane during this time and mostly away from other vessels. In charge of the bridge was an officer of the deck, in this case a second tour division officer, several of whom had also spent their first tour on the *Carney* (officers have the option to remain on the same ship at the conclusion of their first tour) and, aside from being excellent officers, were intimately familiar with the ship. Since the SWO training model was primarily on-the-job, their mentorship was invaluable to us first tour ensigns in figuring out what the hell we were doing on the bridge.

The five-and-dime life meant we were spending a third of our time on the bridge, and without much to occupy our watches when the ship wasn't in transit, we spent a lot of that time in personal conversations. You probably wouldn't believe, in fact, just how much joking around goes on during bridge watch on a deployed warship. To be sure, we were disciplined and we stood a professional watch, but no one can spend five hours on their feet in utter silence. Nor am I suggesting we weren't stringently looking out at the ocean, monitoring our radars, or checking in frequently with the combat information center and the engineering plant. But when you spend a substantial portion of every day scanning the same stretch of water, tracking a handful of vessels on the horizon, and essentially waiting for things to happen, there are more than enough opportunities to talk about home or anything else that young, nearly college-aged people talk about in general. Usually these were not very intellectual conversations. They came out of sheer boredom, but they were also some of the best moments of deployment and a time to bond with fellow junior officers.

Bridge watch wasn't *always* boring. Sometimes, during our many transits across the seas of Europe, there were moments of pure terror, moments when I found myself crossing traffic lanes with cargo ships and oil tankers three times *Carney's* size heading in every conceivable direction, in the middle of the night when all I could see were those ships' navigation lights. There are no roads out at sea. There are basic rules, but these don't cover every situation and it's easy to get overwhelmed when there are a dozen ships around you on a collision course and you need to do *something* to not hit them. That meant knowing what the other ships were supposed to be doing and recognizing when they *weren't* doing that so you could avoid disaster. Without training and the right instincts during those situations, or if you simply weren't paying attention, you could get sailors killed. Thankfully, those moments were not the norm out to sea. Most of the time we scanned the ocean, we struck bells every half an hour, and we waited for our watch to end.

As division officers, spending a third of our time on the bridge also created tension with our department heads, who stood watch not on the bridge but as tactical action officer, or TAO, and headed the combat information center, the tactical heart of the ship. In theory the TAO was higher in the ship's underway hierarchy than anybody on the bridge, which is why only department heads, who had undergone months of specialized training, stood it. But in practice we were never at war, and the TAO, seated in a comfortable chair, had little to do except glance at radar tracks every now and then and mostly read their emails. Our department heads were, on the whole, unconcerned with the time we spent on the bridge or working on qualifications; we were their division officers first and foremost, and there existed a complete disconnect between the amount of preparation and rest we needed to invest in becoming mariners, and the time our bosses expected us to spend managing our sailors, tracking equipment, and doing administration. Often, these dueling responsibilities became overwhelming. But we were SWOs, after all, and being a SWO, everyone in the Navy knows, sucks. In our culture you never felt bad for the guy under you. Our guiding mantra was instead: *I went through it; now it's your turn.*

Officers who stood watch averaged, if they were lucky, about four or five hours of sleep a day, so being exhausted became a natural feature of deployed life. There was an unspoken contest among us, in fact, for who could sleep the *least*. It was almost a point of pride, and officers would loudly announce in the wardroom how little sleep they had gotten the previous night. The more time we spent on the *Carney*, however, the more playing the "tired card" turned into a source of ridicule. The body needs sleep, no matter how tough you think you are, and anyone who accepted taking the watch dead tired was being irresponsible and putting the whole crew at risk.

It was shortly after leaving Cherbourg that I could no longer ignore that something was seriously amiss with Captain Pinckney. I had seen him lose his temper in port and was by now well acquainted with his ill humor, but underway Pinckney's antics on the bridge alarmed me to a more considerable degree. As ensigns it was far from our place to argue with our commander officer; we were both too low in the naval hierarchy and too ignorant in the maritime profession to make any objection when our captain lashed out at us, or anybody, on the bridge. Regardless of our own rank, the captain was *lord commander* on a naval vessel, and it was not within anyone's right, even more senior officers, to question his tactics or his behavior, at least not in public. Given that Pinckney's behavior hardly changed throughout my time with him, I found it unlikely anyone approached the subject with him behind closed doors, either.

On deployment, especially when doing more dangerous evolutions like driving alongside an oiler or navigating a challenging harbor, things on the bridge could quickly become overwhelming, and given the unpredictability of the ocean and the fact we routinely operated in new places with unknown pilots and tugboats, we were not always totally in control of what the ship was doing. The US Navy mitigates that risk by piling a lot of watch standers onto the bridge, much more so than on merchant ships or the warships of other navies. More often than not, this actually amplified the level of confusion when things weren't going according to the checklist, which was not uncommon. So when the plan went to shit because, say, your pilot showed up late or fog settled in and you couldn't see past your bow, it took quick decision-making to avoid an accident. It was expected, despite the many officers on the bridge, that the captain took charge of these kinds of situations so there was no confusion as to where orders came from. Unlike in the Royal Navy, where the navigator announces they "have" the ship when pulling into port and are almost a one-person show, in the US Navy that role is filtered to several watch stations and overseen entirely by the commanding officer.

Pinckney was, to be fair, not a poor ship handler. Faced with difficult situations, he could almost always be trusted to keep the ship out of danger. The problem was that he couldn't handle stress without his anger level going through the roof. Any deviation from his intended plan would result in ridiculous outbursts in which he would, as his veins bulged out of his neck and forehead, pound his fists and scream and curse at whoever happened to be so unfortunate as to be standing near him. For Pinckney, there was always *someone* to blame when things went wrong, and because the bridge was filled with junior officers, that someone was usually one of us.

If an ensign got a conning order wrong (and conning officers are generally the most junior ensigns and thus the most likely to make mistakes) they would be screamed at. If the navigator gave a suggestion he didn't agree with, she would be screamed at. If the boatswain's mates on the main deck below were taking longer than he wanted to get mooring lines on or off the pier, he would grab a radio and scream into it. If the officer of the deck couldn't answer his questions fast enough, more yelling ensued. This wasn't censored stuff, either. Standing any watch on the bridge during an evolution like that became, especially for us new ensigns, something to dread. This was unfortunate; driving ships was supposed to be our point of pride as SWOs, the thing that had, more than anything, attracted us to the surface warfare community.

The captain even unleashed hell, although more rarely so, on enlisted watch standers. I saw him on numerous occasions shout at helmsmen for not manning the wheel to his standard, and these were young men and women who, sometimes less than a year before, were still in high school. Once he replaced a helmsman for not coming to course quickly enough while approaching an oiler for an underway replenishment. "You're making us look like *fucking idiots!*" he yelled. Kenny took our actions on the bridge personally, as if every mistake that his young, inexperienced sailors made were a direct reflection of his own abilities as a mariner. For the ensigns this made any situation on the bridge with him a very poor training opportunity, even though in the Surface Navy, because of the lack of formal training for officers, ships' captains bear most of the responsibility for ensuring their new officers finish their first tours as competent mariners. Yet I cannot recall a single moment when Kenny seriously attempted to teach us anything on the bridge or help us to derive any lessons from our mistakes.

On the bridge, we stood watch on the captain's behalf—it was always *his* ship. In his standing orders, a standard on all Navy ships, the captain set down expectations and rules for how his officers should stand their watch. It included all permissions and reports he expected from us if he was not personally on the bridge, things regarding dumping trash overboard, coming within sight of land, letting sailors work topside in the dark, or starting and stopping engines. Most importantly for bridge watch standers, it defined the maximum distance we could come to other ships (the *closest point of approach*) before having to make a report to the captain. Regardless of the time of day, we were expected to call him if other vessels came too close to the *Carney's* intended track. The middle of the night, unfortunately, was also when Pinckney was at his most ornery, and disturbing his sleep with a report was sure to result in a harsh rebuke: whether we were speaking too fast, too slow, leaving information out or giving too much, it was impossible to get through these without incurring his wrath.

Pinckney also had a habit of making things that were supposed to be fun, well, not fun at all. Deployed life wasn't all work, as no sailor could survive months at sea if they didn't enjoy themselves every now and then. The *Carney*, like all ships, had a morale committee that organized social events like karaoke or movie nights, while the officers, though we were welcome to attend these gatherings, also put together our own social events in the wardroom. Pinckney was well aware that it was in his interest for his officers to get along. On a deployed ship we couldn't go home at the end of the day. We were stuck with the people we worked with all day, and when someone disliked another that could create a pretty sour atmosphere in the wardroom. To be sure, this wasn't entirely avoidable, but if officers' bad attitudes were left to fester and grow outside the walls of the wardroom, the crew was bound to take notice. Pinckney's efforts to force camaraderie among us were, predictably, more often than not a failure. Then again, they weren't really called for. By the time the deployment was underway, the junior officers had already grown close; even a few weeks of living and working together inside a steel prison had made sure of that, and inside the JO Jungle the ensigns already had a place to escape work. We didn't need to play Monopoly with the captain to blow off steam.

One evening early on in the deployment, Pinckney decided to hold a movie night in the wardroom. Our attendance, the department heads made clear, was strongly advised. Only being on watch would serve as a valid excuse not to attend. The captain's choice for a movie was an odd one, a romantic comedy starring Kiera Knightley as a quirky singer-songwriter and Mark Ruffalo (pre-Hulk) as her equally quirky manager. It didn't exactly put us on the edge of our seats, and those who weren't exhausted from watch the night before wanted to get some sleep before their watch that night. Before the movie was halfway over, people began sneaking out of the wardroom, and Pinckney, though he pretended not to notice at first, became increasingly frustrated. Suddenly, he pushed back his chair, jumped up on his feet, threw his arms in the air and exclaimed, "Well if everyone's leaving, I don't know why we're even doing this!" Then he stormed out and retired to his cabin for the night. The few remaining officers stared at each other for a few minutes, the movie still playing, before it was silently decided this wardroom social event had come to an end.

Another of Pinckney's inspired morale boosters was to stage a ship maneuvering competition between department heads. The idea was to pair department heads with division officers, throw something in the water, and have them recover it as fast as possible, a simulation of a man overboard drill that every mariner was required to be competent at. This was an essential skill; people who fall overboard from a ship generally do not have long to live. If the water temperature doesn't immediately sap them of all energy, they're not likely to keep their head above water for more than a few minutes in the open ocean while wearing thick coveralls and boots.

It had become obvious to me at this point that even our department heads, including Lieutenant Masker, despised the captain. But because it was also the captain who wrote their evaluations, it was very much in their interest to let on that they at least tolerated him, if they had any desire to sit in his chair one day. As we discussed our conning strategy on the bridgewing the day of the impromptu competition, Masker was as equally uneasy as I was; given our skipper's normal behavior on the bridge we found it unlikely he would remain calm. At the captain's direction, the boatswain's mates threw a life-sized orange dummy in the water, nicknamed "Oscar" on every Navy ship after the flag used to signal a man overboard. Masker and I, standing side by side and leaned over the bridgewing, ordered the ship to max speed and the rudder hard left to swing around and retrieve Oscar.

While most of our time on the bridge was spent at leisurely speeds, man overboard drills were one of the few times we could truly test the ship's power. Deep in her engineering spaces, after the helmsman had pushed the throttles on the bridge as far as they could go, *Carney's* four enormous gas turbine engines began spinning violently. Inside, marine fuel was being mixed with compressed air to spin giant blades, which in turn rotated two long shafts. These were attached directly to the propellers under *Carney's* stern and below the waterline, huge blades that could push eight thousand tons of steel through the water at well over thirty knots. Behind these were two equally large rudders, against which the force of the rushing water could push the ship's stern in either direction. "Throwing over" the rudder hard, as far as it would turn, while approaching thirty knots was my favorite thing to do on the bridge, as it would cause *Carney's* entire frame to heel over in the opposite direction and watch standers to nearly fall off their feet. Inside the ship's compartments, there was no doubt that sailors and their things were being thrown across their workspaces.

At the time, we were out of sight of land and other vessels, and it was quite literally impossible for us to hit anything or hurt anyone except Oscar, who by this time in his career on the *Carney*, after numerous bouts in the sea, had turned into a rather sorry ragdoll. But, as we all feared, our captain wasn't about to remain quiet while an ensign drove *his* ship. As we came around and steadied on a new course to retrieve Oscar, Pinckney shuffled beside me on the bridgewing, leaned over the gunwale and effectively assumed the conn. Once again, I was relegated to the role of parrot while he drove the ship, and feared that the slightest mistake on my part would conjure up his infamous temper. After slowing the ship and easing her bow next to Oscar, we came to a near-total stop; on the forecastle one of our rescue swimmers readied himself to enter the sea below and retrieve him.

Surface rescue swimmers are a competitive community in the Navy and those who earn that title are held to a strict physical standard. That's because swimming in the ocean is hard enough without dragging a human or human-sized dummy with you at the same time. At the captain's order, the swimmer was lowered into the water from a line attached to a davit on the forecastle. Unclipped from the line, he swam alone to Oscar's rescue and, Oscar in hand, kicked with all his strength to return to the ship only a few yards away, though progress was slow as the swells pushed the ship's bow in the opposite direction. It was at this moment that Pinckney, who had been growing increasingly agitated, entered into a familiar tantrum, even though this had been meant as friendly competition among officers and there were no real stakes other than losing a giant doll. Slamming his feet on the deck, Kenny became enraged that the swimmer was taking so long to get back to the ship and began to admonish everyone from the officer of the deck to the swimmer himself, who was so exhausted he could barely muster enough energy to keep himself afloat. By this time Lieutenant Masker had quietly slipped away—neither of us had gotten much actual driving practice. Eventually our swimmer reached his line and he was raised onto the forecastle, along with the unfortunate dummy. I wondered, at that moment, if perhaps next time the captain himself would not make a better Oscar.

Pinckney, like many of the captains I served under in the Navy, was notoriously quick to judge the people who worked for him, and those officers who had failed to make a good first impression found it exceedingly difficult to return to his good graces. One of these was our supply officer, dubbed *suppo*, who had the physique and facial features of a Ken doll: Tall, square-jawed, and in flawless shape even after months at sea, he stood in stark contrast to our rotund captain. Indeed, our suppo may have been the most handsome supply officer in the Navy. It was perhaps for this reason, we jokingly surmised, that Pinckney despised him. During meetings, Pinckney jumped on any occasion to interrogate suppo in front of the other officers, questioning why this or that piece of equipment or replacement part hadn't yet arrived on the ship.

One afternoon as I stood watch, the captain appeared on the bridge and, through the windows, noticed suppo engaged in one of his frequent workouts on the forecastle. "Look at him," Pinckney muttered from his chair, "picking up weights and putting them down. That's all he's doing. That's pretty stupid, when you think about it." It was a curious comment for a commanding officer to make, especially in an organization that was supposed to promote physical fitness.

There is nothing wrong with a captain giving his officers a good chewing out every now and then, if they deserve it, but it was hard to find respect for a leader who seemed to only see the worst in others, and who blamed everything that went wrong on the people around him and never on himself. Worse, the skipper was squeezing every bit of enjoyment out of our roles as mariners and bridge watch standers. If we had joined the Navy to drive ships, he was making it exceedingly difficult to enjoy ourselves in the slightest. None of the ensigns had expected an easy first tour, but we also hadn't imagined that any one person could make this job quite so unpleasant.

Because commanding officers only serve for eighteen months aboard ships, sailors like to joke that if you don't like your boss in the Navy, "you'll get a new one soon." Perhaps it says something about Surface Navy culture that we are willing to accept bad leaders for that reason. Though I didn't realize it then as an inexperienced naval officer, being insufferable to the people who work for you is not the mark of a good leader. Instead, leading those people to do what you tell them because they *want* to, not because they *have* to, is usually the preferable option.

CHAPTER 5

The Junior Officer Jungle

After some time idling in the English Channel, the Russian sub appeared on our radars. A member of the Russian Navy's newest class of attack submarines, she was making her maiden journey from Russia's small coastline in the Baltic Sea to its naval base on the Syrian coast. From there she would serve as a missile launching platform in Syria's ongoing civil war. To get there, she would be retracing our own transit through the English Channel, around France and the Iberian Peninsula, through the Strait of Gibraltar, and, finally, across the entire Mediterranean Sea.

It was surely unsurprising to the Russians that an American destroyer was following in their wake, as both naval powers ceaselessly monitor one another around the globe. *Carney*'s mission was to gather intelligence about the submarine and her mission. As she remained surfaced during her entire transit, our role on the bridge was to both keep her in sight and in the same relative position to our own ship. When I arrived on the bridge for my first watch with our new companion, *Carney* was pointed south and sailing at an easy ten knots at the heels of the Russian sub. Most promisingly, we were moving again and finally leaving northern waters and the cold behind.

As we returned to more southern latitudes, the temperature warmed and the seas calmed. Within a few days we entered the famed Strait of Gibraltar, one of the world's busiest waterways and our entrance into the Mediterranean Sea. Surrounded by enormous cargo vessels and oil tankers, the passage through the strait was an entirely different kind of sailing from our transit through open ocean. Here, there was no room for indecision—a mistake by the conning officer or helmsman could send us hurling into a disastrous collision. As was customary for more dangerous transits, the captain remained firmly in control of the ship's navigation through the strait.

Once on the other side, we found ourselves finally in the Med and sailing east, our Russian friend still in sight. For days we followed her along the mountains of Algeria, under Sicily and the islands of Greece, past Cyprus and finally to the end of the Mediterranean Sea at the Syrian shoreline. We weren't alone—waiting for us outside the Russian base at Tartus were a handful of Russian battlecruisers and patrol crafts.

Battlecruisers have no counterpart in the US Navy. Nearly twice the size of a destroyer, they were loaded with advanced surface missiles atop their main deck and dwarfed the *Carney*, more like something out of World War II than a modern warship.

For the next few days, we loitered outside Syria's twelve-mile territorial limit and awaited a possible missile launch from the Russian submarine. It was no secret to the Russians, however, that we had followed them all the way from the English Channel (warships are rather conspicuous, after all), and the Russian Navy wasn't inclined, I imagined, to put on a show just for us. Still, the hope of seeing a Russian cruise missile fly into the air and, more importantly, capturing it on video, was the incessant topic of every conversation and brief aboard the *Carney*, and was renewed with every new watch. The captain remained on the bridge nearly day and night, making recommendations to the conning officer to keep the ship in a slow circle around the cluster of Russian ships. Though we remained a few miles away, the large battlecruisers positioned themselves in front of the submarine to block our view. On one occasion we drifted closer and she began urging our ship to "maintain distance" over her loudspeaker.

Through binoculars we could see her sailors, in full battle dress, manning her machine guns topside, and, in what was either a weird show of force or their sense of humor, she began blasting the Russian national anthem over her loudspeaker.

Our little game came to a head one night when one of the Russian ships made a more aggressive attempt to chase us away. I happened to be on watch as the conning officer. Hailing us on the VHF marine radio, she warned us we were violating the Syrian territorial limit. We weren't. We were, however, attempting to get as close as possible to the submarine as we had received intelligence that a missile launch was imminent. Suddenly one of the Russian vessel's forward and side lights came into view, revealing she had turned her bow directly in our direction. She started slowly sailing toward us, our radars suddenly indicating a collision course. On the radio, one of her watch standers repeatedly called out to us in heavily accented English: "You are in violation of Rule 15 of the international navigation rules. Turn away now." They were invoking the "crossing situation" rule, which required vessels to give way to other vessels crossing on their starboard side. By that point she was indeed coming up on us from our starboard bow, but the rules applied only to vessels in transit. The Russians had turned toward us and *created* a collision course in the first place.

The captain, on the bridge to direct the whole operation, ordered me to the starboard bridgewing with him. On a handheld radio, he responded to the Russians that we would not change course. Again they repeated their order until the bows of our ships were facing one another head-on only a few hundred yards apart; I could now clearly see the form of a warship coming into view in the darkness. "What the fuck are they doing?" Pinckney exclaimed to no one in particular. Though he was well aware of the game of chicken the Russians had just initiated, he wasn't about to find out who had the most patience. He gave the order for "all engines back full" and I relayed it to the helmsman. With her powerful rotating propellers, the *Carney* almost instantly backed from the Russian warship, which also began reversing her course. Before the night ended there was plenty of cursing and fist pounding from our captain, whose screams were directed both at Russian gall and at our own watch standers. During the incident, I was as much worried about colliding with a Russian ship as I was about my captain entirely losing his shit.

The submarine didn't launch a missile that night. In fact, she disappeared entirely and, a few days later, resurfaced miles away and well out of sight of us. Not long after, the *Carney* was directed to leave the Russians alone and head back west. The entire adventure took up nearly a month and by the end of it the crew, at least its greener members, showed signs of wear from the unrelenting watch rotation. It had been a proper introduction to Surface Navy life.

Luckily some respite lay ahead. In mid-December, during our transit west, we moored for one day inside Souda Bay on the Greek island of Crete, a breathtaking basin of turquoise water encircled by snow-capped mountains and ancient forts. There we got our first real port call, an actual "liberty call" where sailors were allowed to leave the ship and visit the nearby town of Chania. There is no more exciting moment for sailors, especially those of us on our first deployment, than to feel actual land under our feet after a month locked inside a steel cage. Though some expressed interest in the town's famed Renaissance architecture, these suggestions were quickly shot down in favor of finding the closest bar.

A night away from the ship was a fine remedy to deployment weariness, and *Carney* was soon underway again and on her way to Sicily, where we enjoyed Christmas moored inside Augusta Bay on the island's eastern side and found out that Christmas Eve was not the best night to find open restaurants in Italy. By New Year's Eve the ship was out to sea yet again, an occasion I celebrated on watch in the combat information center making improvised paper hats for the entire watch team. Our deployment schedule had us return to the eastern edge of the Mediterranean Sea to maintain an American presence in the region (we were still, after all, primarily its antiballistic missile line of defense). We were not there for long, however, before one of the ship's propellers suffered a major malfunction. As our only means of moving through the water, this required immediate attention, so we turned around yet again and returned to Souda Bay for repairs. This was welcome news, for this time we earned over a week in port. Although we spent every three days on duty on the ship, it was more time off than anybody had expected and took us over the halfway hump of the deployment.

In late January we were ready to sail again. Immediately after leaving the bay, as we pointed toward the open sea and the captain readied to entrust the bridge to the officers on watch, he received a distressing phone call from the ship's chief corpsman, our "doc." He ordered the officer of the deck to point the bow back at Souda Bay and return there at full speed. A few decks below, a sailor had just smashed his head against a steel scuttle so hard he lay unconscious and bleeding on the deck, in need of serious medical attention we couldn't provide on the ship. At thirty knots we were back in Souda Bay within minutes, where we launched our small boat to bring the sailor to an ambulance waiting onshore; though he eventually recovered from his injuries, he never returned to the ship. The accident could have happened to any of us; he was racing up a ladder well and through the scuttle, small openings between decks that can be closed watertight, at the exact moment the ship lurched upward from a wave.

That same day we resumed our transit and spent the last weeks of deployment sailing in circles in the eastern Mediterranean, training, and conducting exercises with other ships in sixth fleet. Things quieted down on watch; the further east one went in the Med, the less merchant ships there were. I had spent now hundreds of hours on the bridge as conning officer and junior officer of the deck, and was starting to look more like a mariner and less like an ensign. I had gained more confidence in radio too, where I spent much of my time when not on watch. With a few months of sea time under my belt, and the requisite hours spent learning their jobs and involving myself in every equipment casualty and communications outage, I had gained a sort of tacit approval among the ITs. They had accepted, for one, that I wasn't there to bust their balls or take our department head's side. Senior Chief Theroux and I shielded the ITs, as best we could, from the harangues of our leadership and the tactical action officers on watch in the combat information center, who mistakenly assumed that every comms issue was a result of the ITs' poor attitude. To be fair, they *were* smartasses, but most of the time they did their job well and weren't deserving of blame.

If you belonged to the communications division, the radio room was a safe haven. Inside its walls, the ITs were never hesitant to reveal their frustrations about the ship and her crew. They were, in fact, among the *Carney's* most persistent gossipers, and though I tried to dissuade their musings as much as I could, every now and then I couldn't help but laugh along to their wild rumors. Sometimes they even attempted, unsuccessfully, to coax information from me about officers' personal lives and sailors' gossip surrounding them. Many of my private conversations with Senior Chief Theroux, huddled around his desk in the corner of radio, revolved around how to keep "our guys" happy—or at least content enough to do their job and stop talking back to anyone who wasn't in our division. The ITs were in many ways a service organization, supporting sailors with their computer problems and the combat information center with their radio circuits (and ensuring the Internet never went down). At least that's how their chief tried to frame their role, though it was one of our most persistent challenges to convince them of it. The ITs worked in two long shifts; half worked for twelve hours of the day, and the other half for the other twelve hours. Some preferred the night shift; it was quieter then and afforded more time on Facebook, though came with the downside of having to eat only midnight rations, affectionately known as "midrats," the far less appealing version of the galley's normal cuisine. Either way, working twelve-hour days *every day* wasn't just required of the ITs, it was the standard throughout the ship.

In the second half of deployment, because I had spent all my watches on the bridge, Masker scheduled me to stand watch occasionally in the combat information center, or CIC, to finish the crucial CIC watch officer qualification. To an ensign, this was either a blessing or a curse. "Combat," as it was simply called, was very different from the bridge. Located inside the very center of the ship and directly above the radio room, it was the ship's tactical control center from which many of her radars, sensors, and weapons could be operated. Inside, watch standers monitored every aspect of the world around us: some identified vessels using surface radars and thermal cameras, others scanned the airspace for threats, while others still maintained communications links with other US and NATO ships. In one corner, a cramped closet known as the ship's special exploitation space, intelligence specialists analyzed top-secret information. During our first patrol I assumed one of these sailors had left the ship before our departure, only to find out upon our return to Rota that he had been working the night shift inside this space all along.

On the *Carney*, CIC was the size of a large conference room and lined with rows of consoles and monitors. Underway it was continuously bathed in a soft blue light to ease the eyes of sailors who spent hours staring at radar screens. The team inside was headed by a tactical action officer, or TAO, the watch station for department heads, who rotated their watch similarly to the junior officers on the bridge. The TAO sat in the center of the room and monitored two large screens, where tracks from the ship's sensors and radars filled electronic charts. They alone, aside from the captain, could authorize the use of the ship's major weapons. CIC was designed to fight battles; it is where the captain of a ship would go if she faced an enemy, instead of the bridge. In peacetime, however, sailors don't fire missiles at anyone, so CIC acted as a place to observe, listen, and provide navigation recommendations to the officers on the bridge above.

Depending on where in the world we were or what we were doing, CIC could become a place of utter drudgery because, often, nothing happened in the middle of the ocean. If staring at an empty computer screen during a five-hour watch doesn't sound fun, that's because it isn't. It was a wonder that sailors inside CIC didn't all go insane by the end of deployments. At least on the bridge we could see the ocean and breathe in fresh air. Not too long ago, before smoking was banned on ships, watch standers in CIC inhaled copious amounts of cigarettes to get through watch; the older sailors remembered how, when opening the door to CIC on their first ships, they'd be engulfed in a thick cloud of smoke. Today sailors have replaced that with energy drinks and junk food. Just like on the bridge, when things got slow there was a lot of joking around in combat.

I was the CIC watch officer, which during the average watch was not exactly an important post. Ostensibly I was there to assist the TAO in supervising the watch team, though since he could easily do that himself, I spent the bulk of my time shadowing other watch standers and studying for my surface warfare qualifications. Spending time in CIC was a crucial part of earning one's pin; it was where junior officers could learn the most about the ship's many weapons and tactical systems. Watch officers, because they had no real tasks inside combat, were also the ideal delivery boys to and from the ship's vending machine. If there is one thing deployments on warships do *not* instill in sailors, it is healthy eating habits.

I was also lucky enough to stand watch with my department head. Because CIC worked closely with the ITs, who maintained all the communications circuits that tactical watch standers used, Masker routinely sent me down to radio, one deck directly below CIC, to wake up the ITs, whom he usually presumed weren't doing their job. During this time, in an effort to lose the stress-induced weight he had gained during his tour as the *Carney's* combat systems officer, Masker had embarked on a "master cleanse," a diet consisting entirely of a liquid concoction made from lemonade, maple syrup, and cayenne pepper. He did not eat or consume anything else for over a month. I am not sure if it worked, but it did make him even more ornery than he was before.

In March the *Carney's* first patrol in sixth fleet, and my first deployment, came to an end. Four months after leaving Rota, the ship was moored and we were ready to enjoy pier-side life once more. For the next four months the junior officers took full advantage of life in Spain. The ship entered a major maintenance period and for much of that time was an industrial zone. With no bridge watch, I could focus more time on my division and on taking over the cryptography program. I also advanced in my qualifications. By the time we were out to sea again I only faced the dreaded officer of the deck board before I could try for my surface warfare pin. Officer of the deck is a SWO's first major qualification and represents the culmination of knowledge and experience as a mariner and bridge watch stander. After only four months of deployment, however, I was still far from ready to lead my own bridge team. Sure, sailing in boxes was easy, but managing traffic-heavy waterways around the English Channel or Gibraltar required an entirely different ability.

For a few months, though, I could forget about driving ships. My first deployment had been, as can be expected out to sea, a few exciting moments scattered throughout a lot of dull ones. Nevertheless, I was driving warships, leading sailors, and seeing the world; that's why I had chosen this profession to begin with. But as we basked in the Andalusian sun and recounted our first sea stories, the members of the JO Jungle realized something was *off* aboard the *Carney*. Our captain, for one, seemed like he couldn't handle the burden of command, and though he did not have much longer remaining in his tour on the *Carney*, we feared his antics on the bridge could one day put us in real danger.

Deployments were marathons, and to make it to the finish line we took solace in the fact that we all suffered from the same amount of fatigue and the same frustrations. Much of these were born out of the hierarchical culture that dominated the wardroom and dictated everything we did on board, from standing watch to leading our sailors. As division officers, it was clear that the key to success rested in pleasing our department heads, who in turn were successful if they kept the executive officer and the captain happy. It seemed to us, at times, that it didn't matter whether we actually knew anything about navigation, driving ships, or even our jobs. If we simply did what the instructions said, we would be accomplished leaders and mariners in the eyes of our bosses.

More than that, something seemed to be amiss with our surface community entirely. Our role as division officers amounted to not much more than a mid-level bureaucrat, tending to endless administration and rows of three-ring binders. On the bridge, officers navigated the ship without any formal training—it turned out the few weeks of PowerPoint presentations and simulator sessions we had endured at BDOC had hardly prepared us for life at sea. Furthermore, we were constrained by strict standing orders from a captain who had to approve almost every decision we made. One officer summed up the Navy's system of on-the-job training as "the blind leading the blind." Did any of us really know what we were doing?

Early on during my time on board the *Carney*, I was told to take part in "colors," the daily, ceremonious raising and lowering of the flag on the flight deck at 8 a.m. and sunset. When the flag is lowered at the end of the day, it must be folded in a particular sequence and into a tight triangle with only the stars showing, like what you'd hand to a widow at a military funeral. One of the officers on duty that day thought, as green as I was, I should get some practice folding Old Glory along with one of the other new ensigns. Our attempt resulted in a lumpy mess with loose corners and red stripes peeking through the folds, definitely not something I would have given to a widow at a funeral. Even the enlisted sailors on the flight deck with us got a good laugh out of our performance, and good-naturedly showed us a more proper method.

Colors is a longstanding naval tradition and should be conducted, as one captain I served under liked to say, in a "seaman-like fashion." But we had turned that tradition into a joke because, simply put, we didn't know what we were doing. That seemed to happen a lot in the Navy. We were charged, as sailors, with very serious things—driving billion-dollar warships, launching missiles at bad guys, and upholding a long list of hallowed traditions—but sometimes the people doing those things, even those in charge of them, were young and inexperienced. A lot of times that wasn't their fault, and that day it was funny because it was just a flag. But when a young naval officer on the bridge of a warship is staring at a thirty-thousand-ton container vessel barreling down toward her and *she* doesn't know what she's doing, then suddenly it's not so funny anymore.

CHAPTER 6

"Captain, I Fucked Up."

On the night of June 17, 2017, the USS *Fitzgerald*, or *Fitz* as she was nicknamed by her crew, was transiting through a busy sea lane not far off the southern coast of mainland Japan. The watch standers on her bridge that night exactly mirrored the *Carney* (she was, in fact, the same type of destroyer): three officers, a quartermaster, a helmsman, and a boatswain's mate of the watch. In the combat information center four decks below the pilothouse, a team of tactical watch standers headed by a department head monitored surface and air contacts and assisted the bridge team in maintaining a complete navigational picture. On the bridge, a young lieutenant junior grade stood watch as the officer of the deck, and was responsible for the safe navigation of the ship. More than that, her captain had entrusted her with the lives of his crew of around 270 sailors.

Shortly after 1 a.m. that night, the junior officer of the deck stepped onto the bridgewing and noticed a large shape looming off the *Fitz's* starboard bow. Though it was dark, the unmistakable white lights of a vessel's mast and a red light, denoting her port side, were clearly visible. It became obvious, though this vessel had not been tracked on the primary surface radar's display, that she maintained a constant bearing and was heading directly toward the *Fitzgerald*. None of the watch standers in the combat information center had warned the bridge of the approaching ship.

The officer of the deck, alerted by her fellow officer, ran to the bridgewing and found herself in a terrifying situation. According to the international navigation rules of the road, her ship was required to give way when crossing the path of another vessel on her starboard side. The other vessel, in such a situation, was expected to maintain course and speed. Faced with the threat of collision, the officer of the deck ordered a drastic turn to starboard in order to swing the *Fitz's* bow around the vessel's stern rather than cross ahead of her bow. But her conning officer, a newly qualified ensign, did not understand the order from inside the bridge and failed to relay it to the helmsman. The unknown vessel grew larger, and perhaps because she realized time was running out, the officer of the deck quickly changed her mind and ordered her conning officer to turn the rudder hard to port and throttle the engines to full speed in a desperate attempt to cross ahead of the vessel and avoid collision. The helmsman, also new at his post, hesitated to carry out the order, so the boatswain's mate of the watch, a more experienced enlisted sailor, took over the wheel himself, turned it hard to port, and jammed the engine throttles forward.

Minutes before, the lone officer on watch on board the other vessel, a thirty-thousand-ton container ship named the *ACX Crystal*, suddenly became aware his bow was pointed directly at a warship. A seasoned mariner from the Philippines who was intimately familiar with the waters south of Tokyo Bay, he attempted, in vain, to flash light signals at the incoming ship—he knew he was the "stand-on" vessel in a crossing situation and that it was the other ship's responsibility to turn inside his vessel and give way. Instead she maintained course and continued toward the *Crystal* at a relative speed of over forty miles per hour. He ordered his helmsman, the only other watch stander with him on the bridge, to swing the bow to starboard and hopefully create enough distance to avoid disaster.

But the conning officer on the *Fitz* had already ordered the helmsman to turn to port and increase speed, a maneuver that sent both vessels on a guaranteed collision course. Seconds later, in the darkness of night, the *Crystal's* bow rammed into the *Fitzgerald's* starboard side, beneath her bridge, where watch standers were thrown off their feet by the impact of a ship over three times their destroyer's size. Beneath the water the enormous bulb meant to provide stability to the container ship smashed through *Fitzgerald's* steel hull. The force of water rushing through a hole fifteen feet in diameter knocked down a bulkhead and began flooding a large living space, berthing 2, where thirty-five sailors slept in their racks. Above the water, the *Crystal's* bow had destroyed the captain's cabin.

Inside berthing 2, sailors were awoken by a noise like a wrecking ball crashing through steel and by the violent movement of the ship upon impact. Amazingly, others still had to be awoken by their shipmates, who quickly realized something horrible had happened. Their normally quiet berthing, about the size of a small apartment, had turned into a living nightmare. Shrouded in darkness save for small emergency lanterns that served as backups in the case of electrical failure, cold seawater began rising rapidly at their feet. Lockers, mattresses, furniture, and all sorts of other personal items floated among the aisles between racks and made it difficult for the confused and terrified sailors to leave their beds and get to their feet. The ship, meanwhile, listed to port after the impact but quickly swung the other way as the increasing flow of water weighed down her starboard side, making it even more difficult for the sailors in berthing 2 to walk along her uneven deck. They had been trained, however, to egress the space blindfolded and, realizing the starboard side of the space had been crushed by the incoming water, they rushed to the port side exit. The Navy's official report on the incident describes the chaos:

"Seconds after impact, Sailors in Berthing 2 started yelling, 'Water on deck!' and, 'Get out!' One Sailor saw another knocked out of his rack by water. Others began waking up shipmates who had slept through the initial impact. At least one Sailor had to be pulled from his rack and into the water before he woke up. Senior Sailors checked for others that might still be in their racks."

The sailors found their way to the ladder well leading to the deck above and one by one climbed out of their berthing. By the time the third sailor to leave reached it, the water was already up to his waist. Two of the sailors stayed at the bottom of the ladder to help their shipmates climb to safety; by the time the last sailor reached the exit, the water was up to their necks.

Eventually the rising water forced everyone to the deck above. The two sailors who had assisted the others sunk their arms through the scuttle into the dark water to reach their friends still trapped below. Amazingly, they were able to pull two more of their shipmates to safety, both of whom had been completely underwater in the now flooded berthing. It had taken around sixty seconds for the compartment to fill with water completely. Another sailor, the Navy's report describes, also narrowly escaped drowning:

"The last Sailor to be pulled from Berthing 2 was in the bathroom at the time of the collision and a flood of water knocked him to the deck (floor). Lockers were floating past him and he scrambled across them towards the main berthing area. At one point he was pinned between the lockers and the ceiling of Berthing 2, but was able to reach for a pipe in the ceiling to pull himself free. He made his way to the only light he could see, which was coming from the port side watertight scuttle. He was swimming towards the watertight scuttle when he was pulled from the water, red-faced and with bloodshot eyes. He reported that when taking his final breath before being saved, he was already submerged and breathed in water."

The sailors who had made it out weren't yet clear of danger; the water spurted out from the scuttle and began to fill the deck above as well. As they frantically continued to call out and reach into their berthing below to save their remaining friends, they faced an unthinkable choice: seal the flooding compartment and trap those still below, or risk sinking the entire ship. They chose the former, climbing one more deck and closing the last barrier separating the main deck from the rushing water, which by now was close to dooming the USS *Fitzgerald*. Inside their berthing two decks below, seven of their shipmates had drowned. Their racks had been the closest to the point of impact.

Incredibly, one sailor escaped through the starboard side exit of berthing 2, the one closest to the rush of water entering from the smashed section of the hull nearby: "After the collision," the official report recounts, "this Sailor tried to leave his rack, the top rack in the row nearest to the starboard access trunk, but inadvertently kicked someone, so he crawled back into his rack and waited until he thought everyone else would be out of Berthing 2. When he jumped out of his rack a few seconds later, the water was chest high and rising, reaching near to the top of his bunk. After leaving his rack, the Sailor struggled to reach the starboard egress point through the lounge area. He moved through the lounge furniture and against the incoming sea. Someone said, 'go, go, go, it's blocked,' but he was already underwater. He was losing his breath under the water but found a small pocket of air. After a few breaths in the small air pocket, he eventually took one final breath and swam. He lost consciousness at this time and does not remember how he escaped from Berthing 2, but he ultimately emerged from the flooding into Berthing 1, where he could stand to his feet and breathe. He climbed Berthing 1's egress ladder, through Berthing 1's open watertight scuttle and collapsed on the Main Deck."

As the occupants of berthing 2 fought for their lives, the rest of *Fitzgerald's* crew tried to contain the chaos unfolding around them. Multiple other areas of the ship were either completely or partially flooded from the giant gash in her hull, including berthing 1 and one of the auxiliary engineering spaces. The damage caused a rupture in the ship's fire main, the main artery of piping that supplies seawater to firefighting and other equipment, which in turn caused flooding throughout the ship. External and interior communications were disrupted in the forward part of the ship, making coordination difficult for damage control teams. The commanding officer of the USS *Fitzgerald*, commander Bryce Benson, was nearly killed by the bow of the *ACX Crystal* as it tore through his cabin and was now trapped inside. A group of sailors used "a sledgehammer, kettlebell, and their own bodies" to smash through his mangled door, then crawled inside the cabin, where "the skin of the ship and outer bulkhead were gone and the night sky could be seen through the hanging wires and ripped steel." They tied themselves together with a belt in order to create a makeshift harness and rescue the captain, who was "hanging from the side of the ship" and looked like he was about to fall into the sea. Above him, water poured from a broken pipe and torn electrical wires dangled from the overhead. He was pulled from his cabin soaking wet, without shoes and wearing only shorts and a long-sleeved T-shirt. He then stepped onto the ladder well nearby and climbed two decks to the pilothouse.

After colliding, the two vessels remained locked together for a few minutes before pulling away, after which *Fitzgerald* spun around a complete circle. When her captain stumbled onto the bridge minutes later, the watch team was in a state of confusion and fear. The officer of the deck was sobbing. "Captain, I fucked up," she told him. Around them all was dark as radar displays, electronic charts, radios, and other vital equipment were without power. The rudder and engine controls had been cut off and the ship could no longer be steered from the bridge. At some point, a member of the watch team illuminated two red lights on the mast, the international signal for a ship that is unable to maneuver. Benson, the captain, attempted to take control of his ship, but he had suffered a traumatic brain injury in the collision and was losing control of his speech and his movements. He was taken to his sea cabin, just behind the pilothouse on the same deck, where he effectively told his executive officer to assume command.

The ship's damage control assistant, a second tour division officer responsible for firefighting and flooding control on board, was awoken by the crash of the two ships. She ran down to the central engineering room and immediately called the crew to general quarters, the highest alert state on Navy ships. The *Fitzgerald's* sailors, thinking they had just been attacked, manned the three repair stations and prepared to save their ship. For hours they used pumps to dewater flooded compartments and keep the *Fitz* afloat. In one space, too low to pump out the water, they made a human chain and carried buckets of seawater to the decks above for ten hours. Many of the sailors who had narrowly escaped death in berthing 2 immediately joined their shipmates. One stood a fifteen-hour watch in the aft steering room, the only place where the ship's rudders could now be controlled. On the bridge, the executive officer relayed maneuvering orders to get the ship back to her base in Yokosuka, Japan, which they had left only the evening before.

About three hours after the collision, as the sun peeked over the horizon, Japanese coast guard vessels and helicopters arrived to assist the beleaguered destroyer. The captain, along with another injured officer and the sailor who had miraculously risen up from the starboard side exit of berthing 2, were airlifted off the ship. The helicopter was unable to land on her deck because of the severe starboard list from the water weighing her down. Shortly after, the USS *Dewey*, another destroyer dispatched from

Yokosuka, reached the *Fitzgerald*; she sent equipment, food, and fresh sailors to relieve the exhausted crew. Two Navy tugboats then arrived and tied themselves to the bow and stern of the *Fitzgerald*; about ten hours later they limped back into Yokosuka's harbor and moored to the same pier they had left thirty-six hours before. They tied the port side of the ship to the pier to hide the shocking damage to her starboard side.

Beneath the waterline in berthing 2, the bodies of seven sailors remained trapped. Over the next day, Navy divers pulled them out one by one. They were:

– Dakota Kyle Rigsby, 19, Gunner's Mate Seaman, from Palmyra, Virginia
– Alexander Douglass, 25, Yeoman 3rd Class Shingo, from San Diego, California
– Ngoc T. Truong Huynh, 25, Sonar Technician 3rd Class, from Oakville, Connecticut
– Noe Hernandez, 26, Gunner's Mate 2nd Class, from Weslaco, Texas
– Carlos Victor Ganzon Sibayan, 23, Fire Controlman 2nd Class, from Chula Vista, California
– Xavier Alec Martin, 24, Personnel Specialist 1st Class, from Halethorpe, Maryland
– Gary Leo Rehm Jr., 37, Fire Controlman 1st Class, from Elyria, Ohio

Why did an American warship, part of the most powerful fleet in the world, run into a merchant vessel during peacetime? When news of the tragedy broke, none of us quite knew what to make of it inside the *Carney's* wardroom. Back home, the story came and went—reports of aircraft crashes and training accidents are not uncommon in the military, so Americans seemed to readily accept the incident as part of the price we paid for being the world's police. Admittedly, most civilians have little idea what it is that sailors and soldiers of our armed forces do halfway around the world, other than it's dangerous. For the officers of the *Carney*, the media's reports were chilling. We sat in our wardroom, wondering how such a thing could happen on a ship identical to ours. Though we knew no more about the incident than the American public, we had recognized one important clue: that the *Fitz* had been hit on her starboard side, which indicated she may have been at fault according to the navigation rules of the road. It took months, after the Navy wrapped up its investigation and another disaster rocked our community, until we were able to fill in the details of what had happened on the *Fitz*.

The USS *Fitzgerald* had shown warning signs months prior to the collision. Only four months before, she had undergone a long overhaul period where 40 percent of her sailors turned over with new, less experienced arrivals. In the following months, multiple maintenance periods were shortened or skipped entirely so the ship could deploy in seventh fleet, the Navy's area of operations in the Western Pacific, where renewed threats by North Korea and China allowed little time for repairs and training. It was discovered in the Navy's subsequent investigation that multiple problems existed with the ship's surface radars. On the bridge the SPS-73, the primary navigation radar used by watch standers, would often freeze and have to be restarted. The SPS-67, a search radar used to detect vessels at longer distances, could not be tuned from the combat information center, which explained in part why the tactical action officer provided no warning to the bridge in the hours leading to the collision— she couldn't see all the other vessels around the *Fitz*.

The investigation also turned up distressing gaps in watch stander readiness, particularly in their grasp of the international navigation rules and in operating radar systems. It was likely the primary radar on the bridge was improperly tuned, which would have prevented watch standers from distinguishing individual vessels on the radar's display. Most importantly, it seems the officer of the deck had assumed that the *ACX Crystal* and the *Wan Hai*, a commercial vessel also heading toward the *Fitz* from the same direction as the *Crystal*, were a single radar contact, likely due to the inaccurate radar display. In other words, the bridge watch standers failed to identify the *Crystal* on the radar as a separate vessel on a collision course.

Then there were the close calls that occurred on the *Fitzgerald* officers' watch in the months leading up to the tragedy. In May, Lieutenant Junior Grade Coppock, the officer of the deck at the time of the collision, came just a few hundred yards to a fishing vessel, dodging it at the last minute by ordering a sharp left turn. Though that distance would be considered dangerously close by any mariner, she never informed her captain of the incident. Not long after, another officer narrowly missed colliding with another vessel by ordering all engines full astern and sounding five short whistle blasts, the international danger signal.

The day before the collision, the crew started work at 6 a.m. and did not leave the pier until well in the afternoon, immediately after which the ship conducted helicopter landing qualifications until just after 9 p.m. At 10 p.m., around when Coppock assumed the watch, *Fitz* closed in to land and lowered the small boat to carry Navy assessors back to shore. She continued boat operations until 11 p.m. and then began her transit southwest into the heavily trafficked waterways south of the Izu peninsula. Around this time the captain left the bridge for the night, followed shortly after by the executive officer and the ship's navigator.

The entire bridge team, then, was physically and mentally worn out by the time the *ACX Crystal* first appeared on their radar screens near the end of their four-hour watch, just after midnight. Days where sailors are expected to work and stand watch for upward of twenty-four hours straight are not uncommon in the Navy. Unlike in the aviation community, which mandates eight-hour periods of uninterrupted rest for aircraft crews, there is no official process by which Navy ships ensure their sailors receive adequate sleep before starting a watch. It is no excuse for what happened on the USS *Fitzgerald*, but it sheds light on the work culture that contributed to the accident.

There is evidence, nevertheless, that the watch standers on the bridge exhibited clear signs of negligence that night. In the two hours leading up to the collision, the officer of the deck passed at least ten vessels inside three nautical miles and, in violation of the captain's standing orders, failed to report them. One of these came as close as 650 yards from the *Fitz*, and no course or speed determinations were made for any of the vessels, either by radar or manually on a maneuvering board. It is unclear whether this was intentional or whether the watch team did not notice these contacts on the navigation radar due to it being improperly tuned. At around 1 a.m., thirty minutes before the collision, the conning officer and junior officer of the deck stepped onto the port bridgewing to practice identifying vessels at night. For the next twenty minutes it is likely no one studied the starboard side of the ship, where the *ACX Crystal* was becoming visible over the horizon. Around 1:20 a.m., the junior officer of the deck stepped on the opposite bridgewing on the starboard side and saw the lights of at least one other ship about six miles away. She then saw something unusual—the lights appeared to diverge into two different vessels moving away from one another. She informed the officer of the deck, who told her the lights belonged to the merchant vessel *Wan Hai*, which would pass well behind the *Fitzgerald*.

In fact, Coppock wasn't aware of the *Crystal*—her radar display only showed one vessel coming from that direction. When the junior officer of the deck suggested slowing down, she refused, saying this would only complicate the contact picture. Instead of tracking the bearing of the moving lights on the starboard side herself, she trusted the computer screen inside the bridge and charged ahead at twenty knots. Though the *Wan Hai* would indeed pass astern of the *Fitz*, the *Crystal* maintained a constant bearing and steadily grew closer. Minutes later, the junior officer of the deck returned to the bridgewing and saw the dark shape of a cargo vessel, her bow pointed directly right at the *Fitz*. She alerted the officer of the deck, who then made a series of catastrophic decisions that led to collision.

Later, the US Navy would point to a dozen reasons why one of their destroyers crashed blindly into a civilian cargo ship, many of them aimed at the *Fitzgerald's* captain, his officers, and the commander in charge of seventh fleet. These problems, however, were not unique to the *Fitz* or to the Pacific Navy. A year before, a group of equally inexperienced junior officers stood watch on the bridge of the USS *Carney*.

CHAPTER 7
Beer Day

In July of 2016, our second deployment began in explosive fashion. Instead of returning to the eastern Mediterranean, the *Carney* was ordered to Libya, where a civil war had raged since the 2011 Arab Spring. ISIS militants, who had taken control of Libyan territory after the overthrow of Muammar Gaddafi, had been reduced to a small force inside the coastal city of Sirte. It was here they sought to make their last stand against Libya's Government of National Accord, or GNA, an interim authority backed by the United Nations. In May of 2016, the GNA and the US military launched an offensive to retake Sirte from the remaining ISIS fighters. Dubbed Operation Odyssey Lightning, it aimed to finally rid the country of ISIS control.

The USS *Wasp*, a Navy amphibious assault ship, was sent to the Gulf of Sidra and launched Marine Corps aircraft to bomb ISIS targets inside the city, while US special forces advised GNA forces on the ground. This is where the USS *Carney* came in—our primary role would be as guard ship for the USS *Wasp*. "Big deck" vessels like carriers and amphibious ships lack the self-defense capabilities to fend for themselves in combat; this is why they are always deployed with an escort of destroyers and cruisers. The

Carney was equipped with radar systems and anti-air missiles designed to defend such ships from enemy aircraft and missiles. In Libya, we would serve as a shield between the *Wasp* and land-based missile sites or small naval combatants.

Though our first deployment hadn't been uneventful, this promised to be the most exciting mission we'd likely ever participate in as SWOs, who, let's face it, hardly see combat anymore. Best of all, it was ISIS—if we had any desire to fight anyone, it was those guys.

By this time, Masker's tenure as *Carney's* combat systems officer had ended. Newly promoted to lieutenant commander, he returned to the States for his next tour ashore. Masker, despite his rough edges, had probably been the best first department head I could have asked for; not only because he made every subsequent department head seem like the most pleasant guys in the world, but because he had taught me to look at everything around me with a particularly critical eye. Though there was no doubt he would complete a career in the Navy, Masker wasn't blind to the broken processes that plagued our organization. "On board Navy ships," he once told me, "it's like people are walking around with a flashlight, and when they flash their light in a corner they see condoms and dirty needles lying around, so they look away and shine their flashlight in a different corner. What they *should* do is turn on the lights."

My new department head, Lieutenant Schultz, could hardly have been more different. Mild-mannered and unassuming, he seemed entirely unphased by the pressure of leading the ship's most complex department. Indeed, his passive, indifferent demeanor was something of an anomaly for a more senior SWO. Our captain, naturally, took an immediate dislike to him. Schultz once showed up late to a navigation brief with sleep lines on his face, and as soon as he opened his mouth to brief his part as TAO, Pinckney interjected: "Did you just wake up?" Schultz, never put off by the skipper, only smiled. Pinckney was not amused. "You're not doing this evolution," he said. "Find somebody else." Among JOs, the incident earned him the nickname "Sleepy Dave."

In July, we departed Rota and headed east across the Strait of Gibraltar and into the Mediterranean Sea. Our destination was the Gulf of Sidra, where we would rendezvous with the *Wasp* just off the Libyan coast. It was also around this time that the migration of North African and Middle Eastern refugees to Europe had become a full-blown crisis. Fleeing the conflicts of their home countries, they took to the sea in unstable crafts and risked their lives to reach asylum in places like Italy, France, and Germany. Many of these journeys ended in disaster and resulted in the death of thousands.

The *Carney* had, on paper, a "migrant handling" instruction and checklist in case we encountered people floating at sea, but most of us were either unaware that such a document existed or, if we were, we certainly hadn't read it. Such an event, we readily assumed, was too rare to devote any preparation to. In fact, it did befall the *Carney* early on in my second deployment. One day in calm seas, not far from the Gulf of Sidra, we heard an announcement for all junior officers to report to the pilothouse, which usually meant some impromptu training session was about to begin or there was something more serious happening that required extra hands on the bridge. As we scrambled up to the pilothouse, we found out there was a large inflatable raft loaded with people headed quickly in our direction. As a warship, this was a major security risk; after the 2000 suicide bombing of the USS *Cole*, where seventeen sailors lost their lives, Navy ships took no chances with suspicious small boats.

It so happened that Mike, my sponsor when I first arrived on board the *Carney*, was on watch as officer of the deck at the time. Notorious in the wardroom for his animated personality, Mike was known to react to the world around him with an inordinate amount of drama. I once saw him become upset because the ship's toast was too large to spread the single-serving packets of peanut butter stocked in the wardroom, exclaiming that "One packet is not enough, but two packets are too much!" Nonetheless Mike remained collected on the bridge during stressful situations and was a good watch stander, which served him well that day when the captain arrived to take charge of the situation.

Mike's first priority was to order the small craft action team over the ship's announcing system to man the ship's .50 caliber machine guns, the preferred weapon for blowing small boats out of the water. As the raft got closer, it became less and less likely that its passengers meant us any harm: We counted nearly a hundred emaciated, desperate-looking African men waving their arms at us, piled into an inflatable dinghy that appeared in imminent danger of sinking. Our focus then shifted to providing any help we could to them. The captain, initially engaged in maneuvering the ship to circle around the migrants and prevent them from getting any closer, began his characteristic balking as he realized nobody around him had a plan of how to respond to a boat full of starving refugees. The supply officer was immediately summoned to the bridge and tasked with organizing one hundred impromptu meals, while our doc was told to prepare a space on the ship to house, and possibly provide medical treatment, to one hundred new passengers. Meanwhile, the boatswain's mates gathered on the main deck to ready our small boat for launch. Our galley was unprepared to improvise that many meals; instead these came in the form of one hundred, hurriedly made peanut butter and jelly sandwiches and crates of apples, which I'm not sure were ever even consumed.

Our small boat, embarked with a corpsman and armed security, was lowered into the water to deliver food and bottled water and to get whatever information they could out of the raft's passengers. They had come from somewhere in North Africa and were making a desperate escape to the shores of Italy, an attempt that would have surely ended in their demise had they not come across the *Carney*. We were at least fifty miles from land and far from any merchant traffic. Taking on that many people, however, presented *Carney* with daunting logistical challenges. And once on board, where would we take them? It was not in the US Navy's interest, the captain noted to us on the bridge, to either bring one hundred illegal migrants to Europe or to return them to whatever desperate situation they had come from. Instead, we had little choice but to ask for help. A European humanitarian ship that specialized in rescues at sea, the *Aquarius*, happened to be operating nearby. They frequently handled such situations and were equipped not just to house one hundred passengers, but to deal with the diplomatic implications that came with such a rescue. As our small boat continued to make trips to the raft, which was unlikely to have lasted another day at sea, with food and water, the *Aquarius* appeared over the horizon.

The whole episode was a fiasco on the bridge, and the rest of the ship, and served as yet another excuse for the captain to pound his fists and yell at every officer and sailor involved, either in person or on the radio. Predictably, the lack of preparedness in the crew for such a situation was everyone's fault but his own: our supply officer, our cooks, our operations officer, our boatswain's mates lowering the boat, and even the officer of the deck. The debacle also revealed our stubborn adherence, Navy-wide, to instructions and checklists; when sailors didn't have a piece of paper at hand to follow, the bridge turned into a place of mass chaos, with watch standers fumbling about and wondering whose job it was to do what. On the *Carney*, the default reaction to such situations was to wait for the captain to start yelling.

By the evening, the Aquarius had taken on all the raft's passengers and sailed on. I never found out what became of them. Our last order of business was to sink the raft, which was still miraculously afloat, to ensure no other ship would stumble on it and search for its missing passengers. Since we were a warship, the captain opted for the less subtle approach: The gunners' mates tore it to shreds with machine-gun fire, and from the bridge we watched it burn and melt into the sea. With that, we resumed our transit to the Gulf of Sidra. Later, the incident turned into public relations gold for the *Carney*, with headlines like "US Navy rescues migrants at sea" appearing in Navy publications.

A few days later we came in sight of the USS *Wasp*. At forty thousand tons, she was a behemoth compared to *Carney*. Amphibious ships like the *Wasp*, which resemble small aircraft carriers, serve as pickup trucks for Marines and, when deployed, are loaded with Marine helicopters, jets, and waterborne crafts and tanks for invading beaches Normandy-style.

When we first arrived in the Gulf of Sidra, it was hard to imagine there was a battle waging within sight of us. We remained outside Sirte's twelve-mile territorial limit, and though the city and the Libyan coast were clearly visible on the horizon, we were surrounded by the calmest waters we had yet seen in the Mediterranean and not a single vessel other than the *Wasp*. The captain, however, set us straight during a wardroom meeting. "Make no mistake," he told us, "this is an active war zone. Just one guy on a small boat, if we let him get too close before we have time to act, can do a whole lot of damage. Think about what happened to the USS *Cole* … that's all it takes."

In the combat information center, things suddenly took on a very serious tone. Early on during our mission, I witnessed Lieutenant Schultz raise his voice for probably the only time during his tour as the *Carney's* combat systems officer—it was directed at his watch standers who, he admonished, were "not taking this shit seriously." Indeed, both the *Wasp* and the *Carney* were obvious targets for the ISIS militants fighting only miles away. Did they have weapons capable of reaching us? Probably not, but who knew what other extremist might come to their aid as they lay besieged inside Sirte? Around the same time we were operating in Libya, the USS *Mason*, another US destroyer, was targeted by two missiles while deployed in the waters around Yemen. She fired anti-air missiles and missile decoys in response, though both enemy missiles reportedly crashed in the water. It was unclear whether the enemy missiles, which likely came from Yemen but were not officially claimed by any terrorist group, fell short of their target on their own or were shot down by the *Mason's* weapons. The incident, which stirred much conversation on board the *Carney*, was the first time a modern destroyer's weapons system was used against inbound enemy missiles. Our primary role in Operation Odyssey Lighting, in fact, would be to stand between *Wasp* and the shoreline as her first line of defense against such threats. The captain had another point; the likelier threat would still come from small crafts, which would be difficult to see on radar or from the bridge at night. A small powerboat could easily exceed *Carney's* top speed and, if discovered too late, it was unlikely there'd be enough time for the gunners' mate to run topside to their machine guns, load them, and aim.

The initial excitement quickly subsided and, in true Navy fashion, gave way to dull days and quiet watches. These were interrupted every now and then by explosions onshore, which appeared as distant puffs of smoke on the horizon and a faint *boom* that vibrated *Carney's* hull. With no ship in sight and only an imaginary box to sail in, however, bridge watch had ironically never been slower than in war. By that point I had spent countless hours with my watch team and, apart from having nearly run out of things to talk about, we were starting to get sick of one another.

On land, the hundreds of ISIS fighters remaining in Sirte occupied only a small section of the city, blocked by the sea on one side and surrounded on all others by GNA forces. Operation Odyssey Lighting would support Libyan forces' final push against these fighters: while Marine Harrier jets and SuperCobra attack helicopters from the *Wasp* dropped bombs over Sirte, the GNA on land advanced block by block, with help from US special operations. A few weeks after our arrival in the Gulf of Sidra, the Navy devised a novel way for the *Carney* to add something new to the fight. Our ship was equipped with a large artillery gun at her bow, mounted on a rotating turret, dubbed the "five-inch" (guns are generally named after their caliber, the diameter of the rounds they fire). Though designed primarily to launch shells at targets on land, the five-inch was also equipped with illumination rounds, high-intensity flares designed to detonate high in the air, parachute down, and burn bright enough to light up a few city blocks. These, the operation's commanders realized, would come in handy inside a city which, after months of fighting, had been left largely without power. Their strategy was for *Carney* to fire illumination rounds in pre-timed succession nightly and help GNA forces push further into ISIS-held territory.

Our "bombardment" of Sirte, though the rounds did not contain actual explosives, went on nearly every night for the next two months. During the day, we remained twelve miles from land, on station near the *Wasp* and inside our made-up box. But after sunset, we closed to within five miles offshore, unusually close for a Navy ship, sailed back and forth along a single straight leg, and fired our gun continuously. The five-inch was an especially loud weapon, so loud that though my berthing was on the opposite end of the ship, I could hear and feel it as I lay in my rack at night. For the sailors whose berthings were forward of the ship, and closer to the gun, the feeling was even more jarring (the ITs often complained to me about their troubled sleep during this period). On the bridge, we sailed along the same track every night, timing our turns with the gun's shots and keeping *Carney* parallel to shore. Some nights, we could see even more clearly the battle being waged inside Sirte: gunfire, illuminated by tracer rounds, being exchanged over the city, and the occasional Harrier jet flying overhead from the *Wasp*.

Pinckney, meanwhile, had only a few months remaining in his tour as

Carney's commanding officer. Our involvement in a real, no-shit battle, albeit from several comfortable miles away, seemed to humble him; this was a rare experience even for someone with decades of service in the Navy. Though he spent every single night on the bridge during our first few weeks in the Gulf of Sidra, he eventually loosened the reins on his officers, whom he had spent months at sea with at this point. By the end of our stretch off the Libyan coast, his presence on the bridge almost became a rarity. Even in wardroom meetings and briefs, he became more removed, and dare I say somewhat more agreeable. Perhaps Pinckney had finally decided to cut his officers some slack. Perhaps he was just tired of his year at sea.

Carney participated in Odyssey Lightning for over sixty days, during which we did not touch land and left our post only a handful of times to refuel with an oiler north of the gulf. The continuous time at sea took its toll on the crew, who struggled to fill the hours and remain sane. Every week, we looked forward to "holiday routine" on Sundays, when rules were relaxed and, other than watch, work was largely suspended. Most of us first-tour division officers, who had reported to the ship over a year ago, were now close to the end of our surface warfare qualifications, so Sundays increasingly became days to ourselves, until then a rare thing on deployment. For my part, I soon completed my watches in the combat information center and now only had to pass my qualification as officer of the deck, before I could sit for a board with the captain to earn the coveted SWO pin. Much of the crew, it seemed, adopted very poor eating habits to compensate for the boredom, while others increased the frequency of their cigarette breaks on the flight deck. Still, others focused their energy in the gym or on the ship's two treadmills. In emails, we had little to report to our families; each day was almost identical to the last.

Occasionally on deployment, Sundays were celebrated with that hallowed Navy tradition known as "steel beach picnics." These were afternoons of pure leisure held on the flight deck: For a few hours, the crew (at least those not on watch) broke out grills and coolers of soda, lounged, blasted music, smoked cigars, laughed, and did their best to forget they were deployed on a warship somewhere in the Mediterranean. These occasions were essential to the crew's morale. They broke up the relentless work schedule and gave us a chance to mingle as friends and not just as coworkers. The hierarchies of rank were relaxed somewhat during steel beach picnics and any talk of work was highly advised against.

One great benefit came out of our time in Libya. The US Navy, unlike many of our allies, allows no alcohol on board its ships, with one notable exception. If a crew has been out to sea continuously for at least forty-five days, they can request from their fleet commander a "beer day," or what is essentially a onetime alcohol pass. This is exactly what Captain Pinckney did as we lingered in the Gulf of Sidra, and thankfully so—denying sailors their beer day would surely have resulted in mutiny aboard the *Carney*. After receiving the necessary cargo during an underway replenishment, *Carney*'s sailors gathered on the flight deck one Sunday and, in an orderly line, were each issued two cans of beer. Imagine the general feeling among the crew that day, the Lord's day no less, when after nearly two months of ceaseless work at sea, we lifted the tabs off our very own cans of Budweiser or Sam Adams and felt the sweet liquid touch our lips! To complement the occasion, we had turned the day into a full-fledged steel beach picnic. Some sailors tested the relaxed dress code to its limits, arriving topside wearing jeans and cowboy boots. This, of course, had not been authorized, but our leadership reluctantly looked the other way.

The alcohol ban in the Navy dates from the era of prohibition and is, for the most part, a misguided policy. There is a reason why every other navy rations alcoholic drinks daily to their sailors; doling out a little bit of vice can be a good thing. American sailors, instead, replace beer with other equally poor habits: chewing tobacco, cigarettes, and copious amounts of soda, energy drinks, and junk food. When they find themselves ashore, they immediately flock to bars and make up for weeks of prohibition with a dangerous amount of drinking. This has disastrous consequences, as sailors who find trouble in foreign ports almost always do so because they are severely inebriated. Those sailors are sure to find themselves in front of the captain, or worse, in a foreign jail.

In the radio room, the ITs were growing as restless as the rest of the crew. To be sure, my relationship with them had evolved dramatically since I first arrived on the *Carney* over a year before. Among his few pieces of advice, Lieutenant Masker had urged me to ensure that my chief "knew his job," yet he should have gone further and added that *I* should know my job too. My early days on the *Carney* were filled with frustration about getting the ITs to care about what I cared about or, more specifically, what my department head and captain cared about. Often, I found myself at odds with the ITs about what to prioritize in the division; these arguments generally revolved around an implicit accusation that they weren't working hard enough, a battle that, as it turned out, nearly every officer on the ship was waging with their own divisions. As I got to know my sailors and their job, I realized that military leadership was not about "pulling rank" on your subordinates so much as achieving a careful balance between every member of your team.

That meant, most importantly, understanding the perspective of your senior enlisted sailors, those who didn't spend every day in the wardroom with the captain, and coming to an understanding that both your priorities were in fact the same. If the division's leadership—the officer, the chief, and the leading petty officers—weren't on the same page to begin with, there was no way I would get the other sailors in the division to care about what *I* cared about. The military remained, in this way, especially hierarchical, and I learned that trying to skip my chief, or even Tep and Mills, simply wouldn't work. Ultimately, sailors were more likely to follow orders in good faith if they came from their most immediate supervisor, not from their division officer.

This tenuous relationship between officer and enlisted always required our attention. The military, unlike the civilian world, does not hire people because they fit a particular corporate culture—as long as they are in reasonable physical shape and mentally sound, *anyone* has a place in its ranks. That meant motivating very different types of people to work alongside one another and toward the same mission, from eighteen-year-olds from inner-city Detroit to twenty-somethings from rural Texas. There is an old adage in the Navy that "twenty percent of sailors do eighty percent of the work." That's not exactly wrong; some people are more hardworking than others. Then again, some of these kids had recently graduated from high school and never held another job in their lives. Much of our job as leaders on board *Carney*, then, was building a working culture among very young and sometimes very unmotivated individuals. Operation Odyssey Lightning tested that to its limits, as our sailors increasingly began to lose their minds the longer they spent without stepping foot on dry land.

CHAPTER 8
The Master Tickler

It was during our time in Libyan waters that I earned my officer of the deck qualification. When I first arrived aboard the *Carney* over a year before, I was handed an enormous series of checklists that spelled out the knowledge and the skills I was expected to master before I could call myself a surface warfare officer. This system of on-the-job training is central to the SWO experience, and explains why my training at the Basic Division Officer Course had felt so shoddy—SWOs essentially teach themselves how to become division officers and mariners.

As ensigns, these "quals" were our heaviest burden on the *Carney*. No item on the checklists was complete until it was signed by a qualified sailor, which meant we were constantly running about the ship pleading with other sailors for their time and signature. Was it practical for officers to learn their many responsibilities with so little formal training? It sure seemed no one above us was asking that question.

The final qualification for first tour division officers was the officer of the deck underway, the watch station in charge of the bridge and the ship's navigation and, consequently, a position of enormous responsibility. It was only awarded after passing a board with the captain and all department heads, a kind of review panel to test our knowledge of navigation, seamanship, and conceivably anything else related to the nautical arts. My own board, halfway through Operation Odyssey Lightning, was a straightforward affair, as Kenny had more or less made up his mind that he trusted me on the bridge by that point.

When it was over, he made it a point to drive home a lesson I would think about nearly every time I took the watch on a Navy ship: "You may be young, and still pretty inexperienced, but I trust you to take the deck when I'm not there. That's a big deal. That means, when I'm sleeping, you've got the lives of three hundred people in your hands. Don't forget that when you assume the watch." That evening I took charge of the bridge team and the navigation of the ship for the first time and had the right to wear the long-awaited yellow cap emblazoned with the letters "OOD," signifying the officer of the deck. Every surface officer's first watch in charge of the bridge is a humbling experience. Suddenly, it's all on you. I kept my eyes glued to the sea for the next five hours, silently terrified and hoping, *"Please don't let me hit anything."*

The next and final step in earning my surface warfare officer pin, and completing the laborious qualification process, was passing the SWO board, a trial by fire in front of the commanding officer and the ultimate initiation into the SWO community. If I passed, I would instantly go from a baby ensign to wearing a warfare pin on my uniform and, with it, a certain amount of street cred on the ship. There was another incentive: Officers who failed to earn their SWO pin during their first tour were either redesignated into another community or, more likely, dismissed from the Navy altogether. It was rare, however, for commanding officers not to qualify their junior officers; these either had to be *notable* shitbags or give up on the process entirely. I served with two officers on the *Carney* who chose the latter option.

One of these was certainly no shitbag. He was, rather, a respected division officer and a capable bridge watch stander. As he got close to his officer of the deck qualification, however, he decided he no longer wanted to play along with SWO life and simply refused to schedule a board. He continued to do his job but simply stopped caring about getting a SWO pin. His leadership relegated him to a heavy watch rotation in the combat information center, ostensibly as a kind of lesson, but this only encouraged him to sit in a corner of CIC during his watches and bide his time until the end of deployment After his tour on the *Carney* ended, he was separated from the Navy with an honorable discharge. This seemed to the rest of us a flagrant loophole in the SWO community. Unlike enlisted sailors, who have no way to end their military careers before their initial enlistment period, division officers aboard surface ships can simply stop trying altogether and be sent home with a handshake.

Despite swiftly dispatching my officer of the deck qualification, my first attempt at a SWO board was less successful. In fact, it was downright disastrous. SWO boards were a crapshoot on the *Carney*; though they were supposed to test your knowledge of the rudiments of naval warfare, that subject was so ill-defined that senior officers used boards as an opportunity to ask whatever they *felt* like asking. Strangely enough, there was no written standard for what one should know to be awarded a SWO pin.

Though I answered questions confidently enough for the first twenty minutes of my board, I hereafter went down a slippery slope of not knowing what the hell I was talking about. The captain conducted SWO boards like a shark circling his prey; if it was clear an officer was hazy on a particular subject, he would pounce and grill them until they had utterly embarrassed themselves. For me, trouble began when Pinckney stumbled on my ignorance of the Navy's current class of cruisers. I could not answer on which deck the aft five-inch gun was positioned on a cruiser, which direction their radar-guided machine guns faced, nor, most egregiously, why having two superstructures gave them a tactical advantage over destroyers.

Then, the captain homed in on my understanding of anti-submarine warfare tactics, and after too many blank stares and "I'll have to get back to you on that, sir," it was clear this board had come to an end. Pinckney eventually cut me off mid-sentence and told me to "get the fuck out" of the wardroom, which I promptly did. After a quick discussion with the department heads, he called me back in and made it clear I would have to do a much better job on my second try. It was a hard lesson that I had a *lot* more to learn about the Navy.

As September drew to a close, the *Carney* was released from her duties in Operation Odyssey Lightning. Our crew had spent sixty-seven days at sea and fired 285 illumination rounds. The Battle of Sirte would wage on without us until December, when the last handful of ISIS insurgents finally surrendered to Libyan forces. Though we did not see the fight to its end, the crew of the *Carney* could look forward to a break. After leaving the Gulf of Sidra we sailed swiftly back to Rota for a glorious two-week maintenance stop, and never was watch more enjoyable than when our bow was pointed toward home. Even better, it was the end of the tourist season, and we soon traded our steel accommodations for the empty beaches of southern Spain.

Our spirits refreshed, we were back out to sea in mid-October to complete the remaining half of patrol. This time we were headed to the Black Sea, an unwelcomed destination as winter approached. Getting there would take some effort. After sailing back east through the Mediterranean and past the Greek Islands, *Carney* entered the long Turkish Straits, the historical border between Europe and Asia and the only navigable entrance into the Black Sea. After an entire day sailing through the Dardanelles and the Sea of Marmara, in which nearly the entire crew was employed on watch somewhere inside the ship, we entered the Bosporus, the waterway that cuts directly through the center of Istanbul in Turkey and leads into the Black Sea.

The Bosporus is the narrowest navigational strait in the world and is notorious for its strong currents and lack of maneuvering room; one misstep and we wouldn't just run aground, we'd crash into somebody's house. Indeed, cargo ships have done exactly that in the past, which is why you should never buy waterfront property in Istanbul. Because of the volume of both merchant vessels and leisure crafts inside, it was impossible to enforce any warning zone around our ship. As we entered the strait, we were welcomed by the famous Hagia Sophia mosque off our port bow and by a swarm of weekend sailors who made little effort to get out of the way of an American warship.

Despite our firepower, even a destroyer was helpless in such a situation, for what could we do? Shoot them? We simply continued on our way and held our breath, the watch standers on the bridge focusing on the channel's tight turns and the gigantic container ships and tankers passing *Carney* less than a hundred yards away. After a tense, hours-long transit, the Bosporus opened up and we arrived in the Black Sea.

Russia's annexation of Crimea two years before had bolstered their Black Sea Fleet and offered Putin a stronger foothold in the region. Indeed, it was a lot easier to get to the Mediterranean, and to the Russian base in Syria, from the Black Sea than by sailing around *all of Europe* from the northern Russian coast. Around this time, as the US Navy based more destroyers like the *Carney* in Spain, it began to send them more regularly to the Black Sea to collect intelligence on the Russia Navy and its renewed activities in Crimea. That's why, in October, *Carney's* crew found themselves off the Crimean coast, freezing their asses off instead of enjoying the rest of deployment in the south of Europe.

As soon as we exited the Bosporus, Russian Navy research ships appeared on our radars and followed us all the way to Crimea. The transit was slow and frigid, punctuated only by visits from Russian military aircraft. Because of the recent affair with the *Donald Cook*, we were all on edge about how far Russian pilots would go to antagonize us. We watched from the bridge as they flew not far from our mast, like hawks circling their prey. In truth, we were more worried about Russia's research ships, which continuously came alongside us or stopped directly in our path to force us to maneuver, much like the Russian battlecruisers had done off the coast of Syria. A common Russian tactic was to make American ships appear like the aggressor by coming to a dead stop in our path and raising a flag signal that their engines were stopped. We were, of course, still in international waters, and had every right to operate in Russia's backyard.

Once at our destination, we idled for a few days twelve miles outside the Crimean coast, just outside Russian territorial waters. As the officers stood watch on the bridge, the intelligence specialists busied themselves inside their secret space. One day their chief, who rarely saw the light of day, came up to the bridge to look at the coastline for himself. He took the opportunity to impart some *chiefly* wisdom on the ensign. "Us being out here," he told me on the bridgewing, "it's like if I put a pit bull right in front of your yard, and he just sat there looking at you. You'd say, 'Get that damn pit bull out of here!' And I'd say, 'Why? He ain't doin' nothing!' Sure, technically I'm right, but I'm still being an asshole." He had, essentially, summed up the current geopolitical situation more eloquently than any of us ever could.

Topside the temperatures had plummeted, and we scrambled to get a hold of the ship's stock of "foul-weather jackets" to stay warm on watch. Amazingly, the Navy did not issue us cold-weather coats to accompany our coveralls; instead, out to sea, we essentially had to rent these from the ship. These were not waterproof, however, so in bad weather we resorted to sharing the two or three rain jackets posted on the bridge (the Navy had seemingly forgotten that it rained a lot at sea). Thank God we were stationed in southern Spain.

Then again, there was a lot that was wrong with our uniforms at the time, as the Navy was struggling with a full-blown identity crisis since it had attempted to overhaul its uniforms over a decade before. It's hard to find a more jarring example of Navy ineptitude, in fact, than its inability to provide functional uniforms to sailors during my time in service. In 2003 the vice chief of naval operations established a task force of high-ranked officers and enlisted sailors to modernize the working uniform of the time, which was still, at the turn of the century, essentially the World War II-era "dungarees," consisting of blue trousers and button-up shirt, and which resembled as much a 1940s milkman as a member of the armed forces. The Navy deemed it was time for something a little more durable and military-like and ended up with an almost exact replica of the Marine Corps Combat Utility Uniform, with the same digital camouflage pattern, except ... blue. This was a logical design choice, since blue camouflage would help sailors blend in with the ocean and make them undetectable to the enemy or, if they fell overboard, to themselves.

The new Navy Working Uniform, or NWU (and subsequently dubbed "blueberries" by sailors), was impractical for a lot of reasons, not least of which it made us look like Smurfs dressed for combat. If the new uniform was supposed to be functional, it made little sense that Marines and sailors would wear the same thing given the two services worked in very different environments. In 2013, long after they were issued, official tests revealed that the blueberries were not actually fire resistant but would, if exposed to flames, "burn robustly until completely consumed" and "melt and drip" as they burned. This raised eyebrows considering fire was the single greatest threat sailors faced on ships. It's hard to decide, in fact, what is more alarming: that the Navy intentionally issued sailors a uniform that would melt onto their skin in a fire, or that they issued the blueberries before testing how they would respond to fire in the first place.

Either way, the Navy fired back by pointing out that, when out to sea, sailors wore fire-retardant coveralls, not the NWUs, and that even in port, sailors were expected to change into coveralls to fight fires. It always seemed unwise to us, however, that we'd be forced to first change our uniform if a fire broke out, lest we wanted our skin to melt. Our coveralls weren't exactly stylish, either—we looked like janitors with rank insignia—but at least they wouldn't engulf us in flames if exposed to a fire. The problem with the coveralls, to this day, is that its entire stock is controlled by the Navy supply system, so sailors cannot buy them on their own but must request them through their ship, a process that is as efficient as if you had to order car parts through the DMV. Sailors throughout the Surface Navy are forced to wear mangled, faded uniforms at sea that have probably lost all fire-resistant qualities because the Navy supply system can't keep up with the demand.

In 2017, the Navy admitted its blunder with the blueberries and phased them out in favor of the similar green camouflage version previously worn by Seabees and sailors deployed in Afghanistan. These are lighter, more fire-resistant, and won't blend with the sea if you fall overboard. As of early 2020, the Navy was still testing a new working uniform, one that, hopefully, will replace both in-port camouflage and at-sea coveralls (which is, after all, exactly the way the Coast Guard does it). As the *Carney* floated in the frigid Black Sea at the end of 2016, however, we made do with what we had.

Thankfully our time near Crimean waters was short-lived, and soon we turned the bow south and headed back through the Turkish Straits. A few days later, in the more hospitable waters of the Mediterranean, Pinckney's tour as *Carney's* commanding officer came to an end. We held the traditional change of command ceremony on the flight deck in which our executive officer, commander Peterson, assumed his new role as the ship's captain. This was common practice on board destroyers, as it meant the new boss, after a tour as the ship's second-in-command, was already intimately familiar with the vessel and her crew. This moment, and with it the end of Pinckney's harsh regime on the *Carney*, was, admittedly, one the officers had eagerly awaited all deployment.

Peterson was an exceptionally mild-mannered leader compared to his predecessor. A graduate of both the Naval Academy and Oxford University, he was undeniably passionate about his profession and his craft as mariner. Peterson was something of a nautical nerd, and anytime something of note was happening on the bridge, he would be there to take charge and play sailor. During one of my watches, he sat in his chair on the bridge (the captain and executive officer are the only officers allowed to sit in the pilothouse) reading *Farwell's Rules of the Road*, the "bible" on interpreting navigation rules at sea. After what appeared to be a particularly inspiring passage, he turned to me and exclaimed, "That's nautical poetry, Delloue!"

As a captain, Peterson was also exceedingly fair to his officers, a lesson he had undoubtedly learned from Pinckney's eruptive personality. During one of my watches as officer of the deck, Peterson came up to the bridge and noticed a ship was overtaking *Carney* rather closely on our beam, slightly closer than the three nautical mile limit that required officers of the deck to make a contact report to the captain. He inquired as to her distance and, after verifying the radar, I was forced to admit my blunder; the ship's closest point of approach was slightly below three miles, and although the ship was in no danger, I had failed to make a report and follow the captain's standing orders. I had made a classic rookie mistake: No less than ten minutes before, the ship's radar track showed her, indeed, coming no closer than three miles, yet things changed quickly out to sea. Maybe she had slightly altered her course, or maybe the radar had made a more accurate calculation since then. Had Pinckney made the discovery, I would have undoubtedly been loudly rebuked in front of my watch team.

Peterson chose a different approach: Quietly on the bridgewing, he emphasized the importance of the ship's standing orders: "I know there's no way that we're going to hit that ship, but if I ask you how far away she is, you should immediately know the answer. That's your job as the officer of the deck. I expect you to be completely professional, *all the time*, and you should expect the same out of your watch team. This is a dangerous profession, even though most of the time it doesn't feel like it. People have gotten killed at sea for mistakes like that."

Unsurprisingly, the general atmosphere in the wardroom improved considerably after Peterson assumed command. In the Surface Navy the relationship of the CO and XO to the crew is sometimes likened to a "mom" and "dad." Dad, the CO, is the more benign of the two; they are generally the last to arrive on board when in port and do not task sailors directly unless they are department heads. That's where mom comes in: The XO deals with the ship's minutiae and her daily routine. While the CO oversees big picture readiness and the ship's ability to meet her mission, the XO deals with everything in between. Of course that dichotomy doesn't always work the way it's supposed to, and Pinckney acted more like the drunk, abusive father than the kindly captain. We looked forward, then, to Peterson's calmer leadership style to restore order. Yet, in keeping with the unspoken SWO rule that shipboard isn't complete without a little suffering, the new XO arrived and quickly made his presence known.

Commander Tyler Oldman, our new executive officer, embarked the ship during an underway replenishment shortly before Pinckney was relieved as captain, and made a particularly successful first impression on the junior officers. Handsome, young, and affable, Oldman stood in stark contrast to Pinckney's Gollum-like appearance and Peterson's more formal style. He came down to radio on his first few days on board to introduce himself and meet the ITs, among which he immediately gained approval. Though Peterson was sometimes accused of being "bougie" by the ITs, Oldman seemed to transcend the image of the uptight SWO. As a result, he quickly earned the nickname "Ty-Bro" among the members of the wardroom. Inside the JO Jungle, we envisioned a bright future: a cool-headed captain and a *chill* executive officer would certainly spell the end of our anxieties on board *Carney*.

After officially turning over as executive officer, Ty-Bro assembled all the division officers in the wardroom to formally introduce himself. He then distributed to us a document he called his "business rules," which, at first glance, I assumed to be a joke. While I imagined no level-headed person would ascribe to themselves more than a handful of rules, Ty-Bro had just given us at least thirty rules spread across three of four pages.

He was serious, however, and expected us to read all of them, something that he was unable to accomplish in a single meeting given their length. Ironically, one of these rules was "Be brilliant, be brief." He then explained his expectation for total professionalism; being excellent, he said, was now the standard. There would be no excuse for not occupying our time with work or qualifications. Somehow, Ty-Bro made it seem like this hadn't been the case before he showed up.

There is something to be said, even on a Navy ship, for easing your way into the workplace. Our new executive officer chose another route. Over the next few weeks, he inserted himself forcefully into the workings of the wardroom. Whereas Peterson always made it a point to impart lessons to his ensigns, Ty-Bro found joy not in mentorship but in public shaming. A close adherent to the unspoken SWO rule of putting ensigns on the spot, he would assign us random tasks during meetings in the wardroom ("This sounds like a great presentation for one of these DIVOs to make!"). On one occasion he sent an email to every officer and chief on the ship after seeing our disbursing officer playing X-Box with one of his sailors on a Sunday. "Officers should not be playing video games with enlisted sailors," it read, "and unqualified officers should not have time to play video games at all anyway." If some officers carried with them a *SWO dagger*, Ty-Bro's weapon of choice was more like a *SWO grenade* that sprayed shrapnel on anyone in sight.

Ty-Bro's most infamous move was to establish what he termed the "Master Tickler." The Navy had a lot of ridiculous terms to describe its administrative processes, but the one that unfailingly made us laugh the most was referring to checklists as "ticklers." As officers we were charged with managing all the administrative burdens of our divisions and, this being government work after all, we did so with untold amounts of printer ink and three-ring binders. Ty-Bro's vision was to create the ultimate tickler, *the one tickler to rule them all*, in the form of an Excel spreadsheet that would track every administrative requirement on the ship across all departments. Essentially, the "Master Tickler" was the XO's way to ensure that his officers were actually doing their job, or, as one of the junior officers put it, he had found a way to automate his job. It was a bureaucratic masterwork and the ultimate weapon in government-style micromanagement.

The Navy is run not by people but by administration; it solves problems by creating long instructions and checklists that spell out exactly how to manage everything sailors do. This is why Navy ships have a much higher percentage of officers and chiefs than they did in the past—the administration of the ship has become our primary duty. Navigation, warfare, technical knowledge, watch standing—these all come second to our role as low-level managers. Ty-Bro embraced that mentality wholeheartedly and he saw to it we would too. We were not here to drive ships or fight wars, but to administer the naval bureaucracy. It was no surprise, then, that by the end of my tour Ty-Bro and I weren't exactly on the best of terms.

With the end of deployment drawing near, Captain Peterson made it a point to give me another shot at a SWO board before returning to Rota. This time, after scrutinizing every class of ship in the US Navy and poring over naval warfare with the more knowledgeable second tour division officers, I survived the captain's and department heads' questions and was not ordered to "get the fuck out." I passed, and the captain pinned the surface warfare insignia on my dress blues later that day on the forecastle. This was, to be sure, an indescribable burden lifted off my shoulders. With a SWO pin on my chest, I had made a considerable step upward in the wardroom hierarchy. I wasn't the only one; one by one all the ensigns who had arrived on board *Carney* before her move to Spain completed their long qualification process.

For all our hard work, however, something about the SWO training system still didn't sit right. If one were to design a Navy from scratch, we conjectured, they could hardly devise a less logical training method for surface officers than the one in use today. The first tour division officers on the *Carney* were almost entirely self-taught, seeking out what we believed to be the most qualified people on board to sign our qualification booklets. There existed no standard, however, for how these individuals trained us; sometimes a brief chat sufficed to justify that we were, for example, qualified to lower the anchor into the water from the bridge. It didn't matter that we hadn't actually ever done it ourselves. Even the boards, the final step in every qualification, were arbitrary, and had no standard for what questions should be asked or what officers should know. I probably deserved to fail my first SWO board, but then again, I had no idea what Pinckney was going to ask.

No other community in the Navy does it this way. We don't send brand-new officers to aviation squadrons and say, "Here's a book on how to fly helicopters; go figure it out." Nor do we send them to submarines and tell them to ask everyone around them how nuclear reactors work. None of the other military branches have any such system, either, and instead have strict standards and formal training models for officers. In the SWO community, because every ship qualifies officers on their own, there are essentially hundreds of different training systems in place. On the *Carney* we were lucky; we deployed for most of our tour and spent thousands of hours standing watch on the bridge, but if SWOs happen to spend their first tour on a ship in drydock or on one that spends little time at sea, the on-the-job model doesn't exactly produce the best mariners.

A few months later, the holes in the SWO training process would be put on shocking display and, one could argue, cost sailors' lives. At the time, however, our leadership embraced it wholeheartedly. The young officer with a can-do attitude was a hallmark of our community, and neither our department heads nor captain seemed to find it strange that, while everyone else in the Navy learned their job in a school, we were left to figure it out on our own.

With our Black Sea mission at an end, our quiet patrolling of the Mediterranean resumed. There were some brief exercises with other NATO navies, and a much-anticipated port call in Athens, but soon *Carney* was again sailing west for Rota. With Pinckney gone, so was the tenseness on the bridge, making our return home a veritable breeze, not something any of the junior officers would ever have expected from a transit at sea. In early December we steered the *Carney's* bow into the breakwater at Naval Base Rota and moored at our familiar pier. Even better, a couple of weeks' leave was due for the crew for the holidays. With my SWO pin in hand, I shook off the last four months at sea and prepared for the next deployment.

CHAPTER 9

With the Fosties

At the end of March, the *Carney* left Rota behind for her third patrol.
It was to be my last on the ship as my two-year tour would come to
an end that summer. Underway once more, this deployment felt different.
For one, I had become more comfortable in my role as communications
officer, not least because the ITs, after spending the last two years almost
continuously at sea, hardly needed much supervision. Several of the
original members of the gang, the ones who had been in Mayport, were
gone, and new faces had taken their place, but the duo of Tep and Mills
was still intact and kept a close watch on the radio room. There was a new
chief, too, who, although he was no master technician either, got along
well with the division. Lieutenant Schultz, meanwhile, was exceedingly
nonchalant as a department head and generally left the communications
division alone unless something went horribly wrong. I was also spending
a lot less time in radio by the time we left Rota, not because I cared less,
but because I had realized the ITs could be trusted to do their job without
officers micromanaging them.

To make up for it, however, I had fully taken over the cryptographic
program, so if I wasn't on watch I was likely inside a cramped vault,

sorting through serial numbers and managing the program's gigantic administration. Living in the vault became part of my persona aboard the *Carney*. Because of its highly classified contents, the vault was always hidden from view by a black curtain and a locked gate. In this way it resembled a small prison cell, and the responsibility to care for it was akin to a prison sentence. As much as I rejoiced not working in the engineering department, the ship's other junior officers often expressed their own relief at not having my job.

Shortly before I left the *Carney* near the end of this third deployment, the vault chose to play one last cruel trick. One day at sea, the electronic combination lock to its heavy steel door stopped working. It simply went dead, and no matter how many times I or any of the ITs tried, there was no longer a way to get that door open. This was a problem—every single key for every communications circuit that the ship used was issued out of that vault; if we couldn't get it open, we could no longer encrypt circuits and, essentially, no longer communicate with the outside world. And on a Navy ship, that was really bad, the kind of bad where the fleet admiral would take notice. I immediately climbed up to the combat systems officer's stateroom to inform him that his radios and information systems equipment would soon be rendered entirely useless. He nodded calmly and answered: "So who's gonna break the news to the boss?" That meant it was my job.

It so happened we were conducting an underway replenishment at the time, one I was thankfully not on watch for, so as the ship sailed less than two hundred feet away from a thirty-thousand-ton oiler, I tapped the captain on the shoulder on the bridgewing and told him: "Sir, we've got a major problem." I explained the situation and that there were only two solutions: Either we pulled into port immediately and somehow found a technician to take the door apart, or we cut it open ourselves. The engineers on board had an exothermic cutting tool, a kind of welding torch that could cut a hole through solid steel and was the only thing that would do the job. The captain chose the latter option, and within hours the damage controlmen eagerly went to work. Soon the vault's door had a baseball-sized hole where the lock used to be and the sparks from the torch had nearly set the entire space on fire. "Is that open enough for you, sir?" one of the engineers asked me as the door still smoldered.

Because it contained classified information, and until we could hire workers to construct a new door back in Spain, the ITs would have to take turns standing watch inside the vault to keep it continuously manned. There was little for them to do inside the vault, so they made the space progressively more comfortable as the weeks wore on. By the time we returned to Rota a few weeks later for a scheduled maintenance period, they had turned the place into a fully-fledged lounge and were using their new watch station as an opportunity for prolonged naps.

At the start of our third patrol, we sailed north, following the same route we had taken over a year before to intercept the Russian submarine in the English Channel. This time we were headed to the southern coast of England to participate in Flag Officer Sea Training, the infamous British training program that is arguably the most demanding of its kind in the world. FOST, as it is known, evaluates a crew's ability to fight alongside other naval units in simulated combat scenarios, during which Royal Navy assessors scrutinize every aspect of ships' condition and readiness. FOST has no real equivalent in the US Navy, where training and assessments are broken up into separate events over several months. Because of its reputation, numerous other navies, including our own, have made it a point to send their ships to FOST yearly.

Though the United States may have the world's most powerful navy, there is no denying that when it comes purely to surface ships, the Royal Navy, as it has for hundreds of years, still sets the standard. That's a well-known fact among SWOs, in fact, and those of us who have caught a glimpse of Royal Navy ships and the way they do business can't help but admit that we Yanks can learn a lot from the Brits. Their crews' reputation for professionalism and maritime mastery, we soon found out, was well deserved.

FOST would determine, most importantly, whether *Carney* was ready to deploy and fight in war. It began almost without warning. On the first day of our three-week-long assessment, we embarked a veritable army of Royal Navy officers, or "Fosties" as they called themselves, who boarded our ship in mere minutes from a high-speed ferry. Each specializing in different areas of the ship, they linked up with their *Carney* counterpart and immediately went to work scrutinizing every inch of our spaces. It quickly became clear that the Fosties were the highest experts in their fields and that this would be no vacation for the crew.

After our initial inspection, we played daily war games with other participating ships, where every watch stander's move was closely watched and assessed. Every week culminated in a "Thursday War," a full combat scenario and the ultimate test of our sailors' ability to work as a crew. These generally began with the ship being placed in "general quarters," the highest condition of readiness on a warship. When the words "general quarters" were heard on the ship's announcing system, every crew member sprang to their post. *Carney's* decks were then a dangerous place to loiter— move on the wrong side of a ladder well or passageway and you would likely be trampled. Each one of us threw on firefighting hoods and gloves, removed their belt, and tucked their trouser legs into their boots. On the bridge, watch standers even donned helmets and Kevlar vests, though naval officers in full combat gear never failed to look ridiculous.

As the communications officer, I was relegated during these moments to the vault, where I could pretend to watch over the ship's cryptographic material. Here, sealed off from the rest of the ship by a locked door, I waited patiently while the rest of the crew fought fake battles and put out fake fires. This was, depending on who you asked, the best or the worst place to be during general quarters. So much for leading from the front.

To survive FOST, the captain put the more experienced second tour officers on the bridge during the day, when most of the war games occurred. Most of the more junior officers were left to stand watch at night. For three weeks I presided exclusively over the midwatch, from 10 p.m. to 2 a.m., and sailed the perimeter of an imaginary box off the coast of Plymouth, England. Even in pretend wartime, the Surface Navy could be a real drag.

When the Fosties first arrived, I had some apprehension about the ITs' level of motivation for the exercise. Admittedly, there was a general feeling among the crew as a whole that how we performed would have no impact on the rest of our deployment. They had been through enough time at sea since our arrival in Spain that the opinion of a few Brits mattered very little to them. It quickly became apparent to everyone in the communications division, however, that the Royal Navy knew what it was doing.

Down in radio, a pair of British warrant officers showed up on the first day of training and got right down to business. "The reason we're here," they explained to the ITs, "is not just to see how well you can do your job, but how well you can do it if you go to war. We're not just concerned about whether you can patch a radio circuit—that's easy—but if you can keep doing that when there's a hole in your ship and your equipment is on fire. We're going to figure out how to solve problems using *logic*."

On board US warships, we relied not on logic to solve problems but on *procedure*. Nearly every action we took, whether it was an officer standing watch on the bridge or an electrician changing a lightbulb, was governed by a checklist or instruction. But the Brits didn't show up with a checklist in their hand. Instead they wanted to test how the *Carney's* crew would respond to the chaos of a missile or torpedo hit. Those kinds of situations took more than procedure. Whereas the US Navy sought to indoctrinate its sailors to "do what the book says," the Royal Navy aimed to instill instincts in sailors that would allow them to make the right decisions no matter what the conditions.

The Brits noticed, for example, that on the *Carney* the commanding officer personally approved every underway communications plan, the list detailing how circuits are patched to specific radios. "Why is your captain approving your comms plan?" one of the warrant officers asked my chief and me. I told them that it was customary here for the captain to sign off on almost every major decision that sailors, officers included, made. "He should not be doing that," he explained to us. "He should trust that his ITs, the operators, can run their equipment and make their own plan every day. If you find yourself in combat, and radios start going down, you think the captain will have time to tell these sailors how to patch their circuits? If he can't rely on the ITs to make a standard comms plan on their own now, you're going to be in trouble in wartime."

For the ITs, some adjustment was required to the British way of doing business. They were, undoubtedly, good at their job, but they had never been tested to think on their feet the way the Royal Navy expected them to. The Brits also attempted to tone down the harsh language they heard in *Carney's* radio room, where nearly every other word was preceded by an epithet. "First things first," they explained to the ITs on that first encounter, "you don't need to curse quite so much. Do you think people are more likely to do what you tell them if you call them an asshole?"

While I did enjoy watching these British officers attempt their best to wrangle our rugged band of American sailors, they certainly weren't interested in what I had to say. I was no information systems technician, and to them had little business hanging around in the radio room. Regardless, I was more curious about what the Brits had to say on the bridge since, as a SWO, that was *my* job. Our navigator, Mike, caught the brunt of FOST as the officer of the deck during most daytime exercises. For once the captain wasn't on the bridge to run things, as his place during general quarters was in the combat information center to fight the ship. Instead, the Fosties expected junior officers like Mike to make decisions and to take charge of the navigation of the ship. This was no easy feat; FOST takes place in the waters off the coast of Plymouth, just north of a busy shipping corridor in the English Channel. Apart from simulated battles, the bridge team had to weave around very real vessels.

Though I spent the bulk of my time during FOST standing watch in complete darkness or stuck in the vault, I was the conning officer during one simulated small boat attack. Unlike in the US Navy, where such exercises felt like scripted scenarios, the British version was entirely more unpredictable. We managed it in a characteristically SWO fashion: with too many people in charge. Though I was ostensibly responsible for driving the ship, multiple officers, including our XO, were relaying engine and rudder orders to me as we were swarmed on both sides by enemy motorboats.

When it was over, the Fosties had few good things to say about our performance. "You have too many people on the bridge," they told us plainly during the debrief. "You've got a bunch of junior officers who all have a piece of driving the ship, but who's in charge? Then your executive officer is here too, and he's trying to run the show, which he shouldn't be. He's not a watch stander; he should let his officer of the deck run the bridge."

Throughout our weeks at FOST, the Brits repeatedly questioned our model of bridge management. In the Royal Navy, they explained, the bridge was led by one officer who single-handedly did what took at least three officers, and a handful of other enlisted sailors, to do in the US Navy. "Your model just doesn't work as well," one of the Fosties told me privately on the bridgewing one afternoon. "Compare it to driving a car: Imagine if you had one person turning the wheel, another one doing the brakes, another in the passenger seat giving directions, and somebody else in the back in charge of everyone. There'd be too many people doing what one person ought to do."

Meanwhile, FOST was pushing the entire crew harder than it had ever been in our many recent months at sea. Though we regularly drilled on how to put out fires or navigate with broken equipment on the bridge, we rarely integrated these exercises the way FOST did. Here, we simulated fully-fledged battles where our sailors were forced to contend with fire, flooding, and attacking enemies all at once. Standards were high; we were taught, for example, the value of making our beds before battle. "If one pillow falls on the deck and your berthing floods," one of the Fosties told us, "that alone could clog an eductor and prevent you from pumping the water out." *Carney's* crew struggled through these exercises and hardly ever managed a score above "satisfactory," not because our sailors were poorly trained but because we simply had never trained with that level of intensity before. FOST was showing us that we weren't as good as we thought at doing Navy things.

The Royal Navy is, admittedly, a very different organization from its American counterpart. For one, the US Navy has over ten times the number of sailors and hundreds of more ships stationed around the world from Virginia to Japan. It's not surprising that British training is more rigorous given the enormous demand for putting American ships out to sea to patrol the world's waters. But that standard has also created a very different *culture* in the Royal Navy, where junior officers are treated not like ship fodder but like professionals. Unlike surface warfare officers, who are seen as "generalists" capable of managing any division of sailors on board, the British Navy designates separate engineering officers who are not expected to stand watch on the bridge. Their surface officers, meanwhile, receive intense preparation as mariners—after thirty weeks learning naval fundamentals at the Royal Naval College, they spend months at sea only standing watch on the bridge and without a division to lead. During that time, they keep a strict log of their hours on the bridge, just like in the mariner industry, and only qualify as officer of the watch (their version of officer of the deck) after rigorous examination.

That training makes a difference. I interacted often with British surface officers and saw firsthand how seriously they took their craft. The Brits are required to memorize many of the international navigation rules of the road, for example, and can spit them out verbatim. American naval officers, meanwhile, are assessed in their knowledge of these by passing twenty-question, multiple-choice tests. While US Navy ships require at least three officers and an enlisted quartermaster on the bridge to navigate in open ocean, Royal Navy ships do the same with one officer. British officers of the watch, in fact, rarely ask for permission to do anything on the bridge and are allowed to navigate much closer to other vessels before a report is required to their captain. When their ships pull in or out of port and in congested waters, their highly trained navigators almost single-handedly drive from the bridge, something which, on the *Carney*, took a "sea and anchor" team of around a dozen sailors to accomplish.

More than anything, FOST attempted to impart to our wardroom the importance of empowering officers. That started, of course, with proper training, but it also required our captain to step back on the bridge and let us stand the watch. It became clearer to me that our Surface Navy made up for its lack of formal training by putting more officers on the bridge and, in turn, in charge of divisions. What we couldn't achieve through a professional officer corps, we did through sheer numbers and exhaustive lists of procedures. But was that model working?

After FOST ended, our captain attempted for some time to apply its lessons. The officer of the deck should now act, as the Brits had suggested, like a "puppet master," getting the information they needed from the bridge team and using it to make decisions. "You don't need to run around the bridge looking at the radar or the chart yourself; that's what these other people are here for," Peterson contended. Yet despite the British touch, we were still a top-down organization, one in which the highest-ranked person always called the shots. So, even after we left the shores of England behind us, things went back to normal on the *Carney*, and our captain continued to take over the bridge when it mattered most (and when he was there, doing exactly what he had asked us *not* to do). It would take more than a few weeks in England to change our culture.

Our reward for FOST was a few days of rest in Amsterdam which, given our sailors' propensity for making poor decisions in foreign countries, was not a common port call for Navy ships. The next four months, in fact, became noteworthy as our well-earned "booze cruise," a *sailorism* for a deployment with a more than usual amount of port visits. Thankfully none of the *Carney's* crew members did anything noteworthily stupid in Amsterdam, and after getting underway again we sailed through the Danish Straits and into Kiel, Germany, for another port visit. Indeed, it surprised many of us that Germany was even accessible by sea. We set sail again and continued east to the Baltic Sea for a short NATO exercise, where, not far from the small Russian coastline between Estonia and Finland, we were joined by Russian warships, that never missed an opportunity to check in on the Rota destroyers. Our stay was short-lived, and with no other route back to the Mediterranean we returned the way we came: around Denmark, through the English Channel, and back down the coast of Europe to Spain.

By now, a new group of ensigns was arriving on board to replace the veteran first tour officers (my own tour on the *Carney* would soon come to an end). So, just as I was finally getting good at it, I began turning over my responsibilities as communications officer to somebody else. That was the unfortunate nature of leadership on board ships; if you didn't like your boss in the Navy, as I was once told, just wait a bit. For my remaining few months on board, I would act solely as the cryptographic manager. The best part about that job, although it did mostly suck, was that my leadership knew nothing about how it worked, so more or less left me alone entirely. It kept me employed, but I certainly had a lot more time on my hands now that I no longer had to answer for every communications problem on board.

In July, we crossed the Mediterranean and entered the Black Sea once more, this time for an exercise with the Ukrainian Navy called "Sea Breeze" (which, incidentally, was a shit name for a war game). We docked in Odessa, Ukraine's version of a seaside resort, where we learned we'd host a reception for Navy dignitaries on the *Carney* the next day and which the head of US sixth fleet, Vice Admiral Grady, would attend. As the captain of one of the Rota destroyers, the Mediterranean's busiest ships, it was fair to assume that Peterson was on the admiral's radar. A thorough Navy man, Peterson knew the importance of making a good impression and realized that the *Carney* was in no shape to receive a three-star admiral upon our arrival in Odessa. Steel ships rusted quickly in seawater, and though we regularly washed the decks with fresh water, the ship was showing her age after two months on deployment.

So as soon as Carney was moored, the captain ordered all hands not on watch to the pier to give her a makeover. Instead of a night off, nearly the entire crew spent the evening rolling grey paint onto the *Carney's* hull, and only the side of the ship, of course, visible from the pier. "Imagine the impression this'll make when the admiral sees her," Peterson said in a dubious attempt at motivation as he watched us, paint rollers in hand, struggle not to fall into the water below. At least it was better than being underway.

Though life at sea had by then taken on a maddening rhythm, my final deployment on the *Carney* held one more surprise. One night, as we sailed somewhere in the eastern Mediterranean, one of the other junior officers poked his head into my rack and shook me awake. Someone had called the wardroom, he explained, and had summoned me to the bridge. I asked him, with some amount of irritation, what they wanted, as I had just fallen asleep in preparation for the 2 a.m. watch that night.

"It's the navigator," he answered. "He says we have a medical emergency and you're going to be the small boat officer." I realized this was no time for protest—I threw on my uniform and hurried up to the nearly pitch-dark bridge where Mike, our navigator, directed me to the electronic chart. He told me we were sending the small boat to shore on Cyprus, the closest land, and pointed to the route I should take on the chart and to the lights and buoys that would guide me to the nearest harbor. The captain, who had been quietly sitting in his chair staring at a large, dark landmass in front of our bow, turned toward us. "We've had a medical emergency," he explained. "When you get inside that harbor there'll be an ambulance waiting; Doc's coming with you so you don't need to worry about any of that. Just get the boat there safely. You know what you're doing?" I nodded, grabbed a handheld VHF radio and climbed down to the main deck.

Outside the air was warm and the sea calm, the boat deck illuminated by a harsh yellow light that completely obliterated my night vision. As the boatswain's mates readied one of our seven-meter inflatable boats for launch, their chief threw me a lifejacket. I expected a horrifying scene, someone passed out or bloody, lying in a stretcher and clinging to life. Instead, I saw one of our cooks, the one who worked in the wardroom's galley and made the officers' meals, dressed in civilian clothes. He appears composed, not looking at all like someone suffering a medical emergency. One of our corpsmen stood beside him. I didn't ask questions—my job was to get him to shore; I could figure out the rest later.

As the landmass ahead of us grew larger, the officer of the deck on the bridge above ordered the boatswain's mates to "place the RHIB at the rail," to unstrap it and swing it toward the ship's gunwales so we could embark. Along with a coxswain, an engineer, a rescue swimmer, the corpsman, and the cook himself, I stepped off *Carney* and onto the small boat, which was affectionately known as "Betty" by the crew. The bridge then ordered us to lower the boat into the sea and, as its keel made contact with the water, the engineer started the engine, we untied Betty from the ship, and were off toward Cyprus.

Carney, visible only by her green and white navigation lights in the darkness, shrank rapidly behind us. Nobody spoke, so I turned to the cook. "You all right?" I asked. He only nodded and forced a smile. I looked for a blinking green buoy and pointed it out to our coxswain, who skillfully navigated our small vessel through the breakwater and into an unknown harbor. I had no idea what city we were in, or even what language they spoke in Cyprus. On the other side of the harbor, past the piers, an ambulance was waiting for us, as promised. After mooring the small boat, the corpsman took the cook by the arm and hurried toward it. That's when I overheard their conversation and the mystery was finally revealed.

The cook, earlier that night, had forced down a near-bottle's worth of aspirin in an apparent suicide attempt. Quickly wishing to reverse his decision, he rushed to medical and confessed the act to the corpsman on duty. The ship's entire medical team, alerted of the emergency, did their best to induce at least some of the pills out of the patient's stomach. With access to only limited equipment, however, the chief corpsman, and our captain, believed it prudent to send the cook to the nearest hospital to pump the rest out.

Both sailors then climbed into the ambulance and drove away, leaving the rest of my small crew rather dumbfounded. After failing to reach the Carney with my weak handheld radio, I turned to them: "Let's go back, I guess." We could no longer see the ship from where we were, the sky was too dark and the lights onshore too bright, so we just drove the reciprocal course we originally steered, and a few minutes later three navigation lights, one green and two white, came into view, and soon after we recognized the familiar form of a destroyer. After we were hoisted back onto the ship, I realized it was just before 2 a.m., just in time to head back to the bridge and start my watch. On the way, I stopped in the wardroom and, like a good SWO, shook off the exhaustion and gulped down a tepid cup of coffee.

This had, unfortunately, not been the only similar incident we experienced on the Carney.

The suicide rate among active-duty members of the Navy has more than doubled since 2006—in 2019 it climbed to twenty-two suicides per one hundred thousand sailors, well above the national average. The question of *why* is a complex one, and I will not attempt to do it justice here, though nearly every service member has been directly or indirectly affected by suicide. In my own experience, this very real problem is complicated by the contention held by many sailors that attempts or intimations of suicide are often staged. In Navy parlance this is known as "pulling the crazy card," or faking suicidal thoughts to get out of deployment or duty at sea. Any mention of suicide to medical personnel is taken very seriously in the Navy and is likely, in any situation, to get you sent home and to a mental health professional. Sailors know that and, like some twisted loophole, are known to abuse it. Aside from the incident in Cyprus (that sailor returned to the ship not long after), I saw two other crew members sent off the ship during my tour on the *Carney* for expressing suicidal thoughts. One of them happened to be a new guy in my division; he lasted about a month on deployment before being sent back to Rota.

The other ITs in the division had their own explanation. What we had witnessed, they assured me, was a classic case of "pulling the crazy card." This guy had already proven himself to be a shitbag, they contended; he sat behind others as they worked and made no effort to learn his job, boasting about his prospects back home and openly regretting his choice of career in the Navy. In the world of sailor justice, this newbie had broken every law and gotten away with it. And now, he had left his division high and dry, with one less worker to perform maintenance and stand watch, and at the start of a patrol, no less. He was, following his departure, not even worth mentioning within radio.

Regardless of that sailor's intentions, he had failed to earn the benefit of the doubt from his shipmates, who unhesitatingly branded him as the kind of sailor who was unwilling to work or put others before himself. The other sailor who left the ship under the same circumstances, a watch stander in the combat information center, was similarly excommunicated from the *Carney* community. The lesson was clear: if we can hack it, so can you.

There is no doubt that deployments take a mental toll on every sailor. No one can avoid the crushing loneliness of life away from home and aboard a steel vessel floating at sea for months. How we experience that individually and how we express it, however, continues to be misunderstood by many of us in the Navy.

In August of 2017, the *Carney* was back in Spain, and my first tour was over. The ship, even after spending at least half of the previous two years at sea, was still the imposing war machine I had first embarked in Mayport, Florida, albeit with a few more rust spots. Since then, she had sailed the Atlantic, the Baltic, the North Sea, the Black Sea, and had crossed the Mediterranean over a dozen times. She had moored in Spain, Italy, Greece, France, England, Israel, the Netherlands, Germany, and even Ukraine. Hundreds of sailors, and two captains, had departed or joined her crew. For us, the ship was a strange source of scorn and affection, a place of long days, exhausting watches, ceaseless stress, a few terrifying moments, and the petty squabbles of three hundred people confined together inside steel compartments. It was also our home, and for that, stepping off the brow of the USS *Carney* for the last time elicited a peculiar mix of elation and regret.

When sailors are on deployment, there is little else they look forward to more than going home. When that day finally comes, though, suddenly your days aren't driven by a watch schedule and you're no longer surrounded by your best friends all the time. Regardless of what your life is like at home, your shipmates become your family at sea. Deployment sucks, but because it sucks, the good moments, like the barbecues on the flight deck and the nights in foreign ports, are as equally joyous as the bad ones are painful. The end of my first tour in the Navy gave way to that familiar emptiness—I had been looking forward to it for so long that when I actually found myself on a flight to America, I was overwhelmed by that familiar emptiness, like I was leaving an experience behind that I wasn't likely to ever find again.

CHAPTER 10
Shift the Rudder

Shortly before my departure from the *Carney*, as we sailed in circles somewhere in the Mediterranean Sea, we heard a peculiar report about an incident involving a US destroyer, the USS *Fitzgerald*, and a cargo ship off the coast of Japan. Though the details at the time were hazy, we gathered the two had somehow collided, that *Fitzgerald* had been left with an enormous gash in her hull, and that seven of her sailors were missing. Perhaps I was naive not to immediately put those pieces together; the hole in her hull was exactly where one of her berthing spaces was located, and those sailors hadn't fallen overboard or mysteriously disappeared. They were dead.

While we waited for the Navy's investigation, I mostly stopped thinking about the *Fitzgerald*. A short time after the incident I left the *Carney* and Spain and didn't want to worry about ships or going out to sea for a while. Surely someone was to blame, and surely something like that would never happen while *I* was on watch, I assumed. In late August I arrived in Newport, Rhode Island, to start the Advanced Division Officer Course, a five-week class to prepare junior officers for their second sea tour in the Surface Navy.

That night news reports poured in about another collision involving a Navy destroyer, this time off the coast of Singapore. Ten sailors missing. This time there was no question what that meant.

The next day I reported to the Surface Warfare Officer School Command, a brick building overlooking the Narragansett Bay and nearly adjacent to the Navy's Officer Candidate School, where I had commissioned over two years before. None of us though, lieutenant junior grades fresh off their first tour on board Navy ships, felt much like reminiscing. Something inexplicable and terrifying was happening, and we still didn't know quite what the hell it was. That morning the school's commanding officer, Captain Scott Robertson, assembled all students and staff in the building's auditorium. He knew the same facts we did: The USS *John S. McCain*, an *Arleigh Burke*-class destroyer, had collided with a tanker vessel near the Singapore Strait. One of the aft berthings had flooded and, in some twisted repeat of the *Fitzgerald* tragedy, ten sailors had drowned.

"There is a problem in our Navy right now," he explained to the hundreds of surface warfare officers seated attentively before him, "and we're going to figure it out. Mark my words, things need to change in our community. We are going to *shift the rudder*" (this was a reference to a conning order in which a helmsman swings the rudder in the opposite direction to quickly change direction). Here was a bold claim; the man in charge of the Surface Navy's training hub was announcing that our community was royally screwed up. He put into question everything we had learned as SWOs and, with it, the very insignia we wore on our uniforms.

I quickly learned the feeling was mutual among my peers and that my experience on the USS *Carney* wasn't unique. Fatigue, lack of training, lack of standards in our qualifications, and crippling institutional thinking in our wardrooms; I heard the same stories from nearly every young officer around me. They had served on destroyers, cruisers, amphibious ships, minesweepers, even littoral combat ships, and collectively had sailed through much of the world's waters. We all welcomed the captain's remarks—something was indeed screwed up in the Surface Navy and we hoped this latest catastrophe would signal a change.

Until we could figure out what that was, our classes began as scheduled.

Dressed in our service khaki uniforms, we spent our days staring at PowerPoint presentations and reviewing, for the most part, what we had already learned for our SWO boards. Ship handling sessions in the virtual reality simulator were more fruitful; though, embarrassingly enough, I performed abysmally in my final assessment, crashing my ship either onto a pier or another vessel three times in one day. My instructor wasn't much help. "Why did you do that?" he simply asked. I was allowed another attempt, and passed, but was alarmed nonetheless that I could still fail basic tests of ship driving, especially when real ships were crashing into other real ships in our Navy.

An instructor in our navigation class mused one day about the impact the *Fitz* and *McCain* tragedies were already having on our community. "We've talked about this a lot here as instructors," he explained, "and I think that, as a profession, we need to answer a very serious question: What are SWOs? Are we mariners, or are we warfighters? Let's put it this way, is our job to drive ships that happen to have weapons on them, or is it to operate weapons that happen to be on ships?"

SWOs had always been touted as *generalists*, versatile professionals who knew as much about navigation at sea as they did about launching missiles and running an engineering plant. But here, at the heart of our collective culture in Newport, junior officers and even captains were questioning that basic tenet. The surface warfare officer community had been thrown into a full-fledged identity crisis, and the obvious remedy, it seemed to us at the time, was that we needed to get back to just being mariners. Wasn't this central to the Navy to begin with? Surely this was the "rudder shift" the school's commanding officer had suggested.

Meanwhile, in Singapore, Navy divers were still struggling to enter the flooded compartments of the USS *John S. McCain*. One of her berthings had been crushed so badly that the resulting mass of crumpled steel and debris made progress slow and dangerous. Inside lay the bodies of ten sailors.

The captain of the USS *John S. McCain* stepped onto the bridge just after 1 a.m. Halfway through a six-month deployment in the western Pacific, his ship neared the entrance of the busy shipping lane south of Singapore, where the crew was scheduled to begin a port call later that morning. Sailors find different ways to break up the long monotony of months at sea, and getting over the mid-deployment "hump" is something everyone looks forward to. Though the *McCain* was hours from entering the Singapore Strait, her captain wanted to supervise the bridge team as the ship reached the notoriously congested waterway between Malaysia and Indonesia, a giant bottleneck through which thousands of vessels squeezed through every day to enter a narrow lane marked on their chart. The moon had set and the sky was overcast and especially dark that night; on the *McCain's* bridge they could only see the white, red, and green lights of the dozens of container ships, tankers, and fishing vessels sailing in every conceivable direction around them. The captain knew his officers could use the backup. He also knew that two months before, the USS *Fitzgerald*, another destroyer that shared their homeport of Yokosuka, Japan, had collided with a cargo ship in far less challenging conditions.

At 4:30 a.m., the executive officer stepped onto the bridge to provide further assistance. Shortly before, additional navigation watch standers had arrived, including the ship's navigator, as the ship closed to within ten nautical miles from land. The sun would not rise for another two and a half hours. At 5:19 the ship entered the westward traffic lane inside the Singapore Strait; all around her vessels left the South China Sea behind and converged to enter the narrow waterway. Despite the presence of additional sailors, the captain had not yet called up the "sea and anchor detail," the full complement of navigation and engineering watch standers required when ships enter port or operate very close to land.

Around this time, the captain noticed that the helmsman was struggling to maintain a steady course while simultaneously manipulating the ship's engine throttles. He ordered an additional watch stander, a "lee helmsman," to operate the throttles on another console so the helmsman could focus his attention on manning the wheel and keeping the ship on course. The *McCain*, though nearly twenty-five years old, had been refitted with the latest control console on the bridge. Other than the physical wheel to turn the rudder, almost all other controls, including the throttles, resided on two separate, adjacent touchscreens. This complex system, known as the Integrated Bridge and Navigation System, would play a central role in the looming disaster.

The young sailor at the wheel that night had finished Navy boot camp only five months before and had driven the ship by himself only six times. He was mostly unfamiliar with the convoluted digital dials and buttons that populated the screen in front of him. After the captain's order to split steering and speed into two separate stations, a new watch stander posted himself behind the screen directly adjacent to the helmsman. The boatswain's mate of the watch, who directly supervised these two sailors, leaned over the helmsman's shoulder and attempted to transfer throttle control to the other screen. Suddenly, the helmsman noticed that the rudder's indicator did not move when he turned the wheel (because of the force of current and winds, a helmsman must make constant small adjustments on the wheel to keep a ship steady).

Just like he had been trained, he announced to everyone on the bridge that he had just experienced a "loss of steering," the most basic casualty that bridge watch standers train for in the Navy, and which would have immediately raised alarm bells among the officers standing on the other side of the steering console, at the time focused on navigating their ship into a difficult strait. They immediately ordered the boatswain's mate of the watch to announce the casualty over the ship's speakers in order to alert sailors below to rush to aft steering, the small space directly above the rudders where a secondary console allowed them to steer the ship if the bridge controls failed.

But the bridge hadn't actually lost control of steering. When transferring throttle control to the other screen, the boatswain's mate of the watch had inadvertently transferred both throttles *and* steering, so that now the lee helmsman, who stood right next to the helmsman, was the one who could turn the ship at *his* console. Nobody realized this and continued under the assumption that steering was lost on the bridge entirely. To understand what happened next requires some explanation of the physics of driving ships, though this is necessary to comprehend how, less than four minutes later, a tanker's bow punctured through the *McCain's* hull.

Before the captain's order to transfer speed control, the helmsman had kept the rudder turned slightly to the right to maintain course, a phenomenon caused by current pushing on the ship. When control was transferred to the lee helmsman, the ship's enormous rudders automatically returned to their centerline position. This caused the ship, which before had been sailing in a straight line, to begin veering slightly to the left. At the same time a six-hundred-foot, thirty-thousand-ton tanker called the *Alnic MC* was sailing just ahead of and left of the *McCain*, but at a slower speed. Since both vessels were headed into the strait, the *McCain* had originally intended to overtake the *Alnic* and leave her behind.

After the loss of steering was announced, and realizing steering control would have to be transferred to the other station above the rudders, the captain ordered the ship slowed to ten knots. Though they perceived a lack of steering control, the watch standers knew they still had control of the throttles, and thus the ship's speed. This is where yet another mistake, caused by the overly complex IBNS, sealed the ship's fate. When attempting to transfer speed as originally ordered by the captain, the boatswain's mate of the watch transferred only a single shaft (a destroyer has two shafts, each with one set of propellers that moves the ship through the water). In rushing to announce the loss of steering, none of the watch standers ensured that both shafts were properly "coupled," so that moving one dial on the touchscreen would change the speed for both shafts. The lee helmsman, then, inadvertently slowed only one shaft, while the other still churned away at its original speed, meaning the ship slowed slightly but not to the speed of ten knots the captain intended. Meanwhile, the *McCain* continued to overtake the *Alnic MC* while simultaneously turning slowly toward her.

The officers failed to fully understand what was happening to their ship, why she was not slowing down more or why the compass showed her bow turning to the left. It is unclear whether they were aware of the *Alnic* besides them and how the two ships were moving in relation to one another. The captain further ordered their speed reduced to five knots, but again *McCain* continued charging ahead faster than he wanted. Minutes after the announcement of the loss of steering was made throughout the ship, sailors reached the aft steering room and took control of the rudders at their station, but a watch stander on the bridge mistakenly sent control back to the bridge almost immediately, thinking he was offering control to the sailors in aft steering. The misunderstanding was quickly cleared up and the aft steering room regained control, but thirty seconds of this back-and-forth only prolonged the *McCain's* uncommanded drift toward the *Alnic*. Even worse, the wheel in aft steering was, unbeknownst to those watch standers, turned all the way to the left when they initially took control, which caused the ship to veer even more sharply toward the *Alnic* for a few seconds, before the wheel could be righted. Meanwhile, the lee helmsman on the bridge finally realized that he was not controlling both shafts. He corrected this on his console and the ship now began actually slowing to five knots, but by then the *McCain*, after a few minutes of turning into *Alnic's* path, was nearly in front of the *Alnic*.

In the roughly four minutes during which these events transpired, the captain never had full control of speed or steering, nor did he understand the mistakes his watch standers were making and how these were affecting the ship. Though aft steering eventually gained full control and turned the rudder back to the right to steady the *McCain*, the momentum of the ship turning left was too powerful to immediately overcome and, combined with the sudden slowing of the ship to five knots, put both vessels on a collision course. At 5:24, the night still entirely dark and moonless, the *Alnic's* bow rammed into the *McCain's* port side. Just like when the *Crystal* collided with the *Fitzgerald*, her bulbous bow struck the hull of the *McCain* below the waterline, this time directly into a small berthing aft of the ship. On the bridge and in the aft steering room, watch standers were thrown to the deck by the impact.

What happened next follows like a morbid repeat of the events of the *Fitzgerald* tragedy. Sailors throughout the ship felt the collision and believed they had run aground or been attacked. On the bridge, officers sounded the collision alarm and ordered the crew to general quarters. They illuminated two red lights on the mast to indicate their ship was "not under command" and announced the collision on the VHF marine radio to warn the countless vessels still surrounding them. Locked together for almost ten minutes after the collision, both ships continued drifting helplessly, in the middle of the night, into the busiest shipping route in the world. The captain immediately requested assistance from Singapore's harbor to get his ship back to port. Most electronic systems inside the pilothouse went dark.

At the opposite end of the ship, berthing 5 had just been crushed like a soda can by the thick bow of the *Alnic*. I knew berthing 5 on a destroyer intimately; it was designated as the JO Jungle on the *Carney* and was where I and all the other male ensigns slept. It contained about twenty racks and lockers arranged in small haphazard rows, a small lounge area with a couch and TV, and a bathroom with a single shower and toilet. The *Alnic* created a hole twenty-eight feet wide in the *McCain* and crumpled berthing 5 to a third of its original size. Unlike on the *Fitz*, where water rushed in from an adjacent space, the berthing was hit directly and likely flooded in under a minute.

Twelve sailors were inside at the time. Only two made it out. One had just started climbing the stairs leading out of the berthing to go on watch when the *Alnic* crashed through only feet away. He was knocked down to the deck, where seawater and fuel from a nearby punctured tank quickly pooled around him. After scrambling to his feet, he had no time to check on his shipmates before the rising water forced him up the stairs to the deck above.

The other sailor managed a miraculous escape. Awoken by the crash, the Navy's report on the accident explains, he heard "the pushing of metal" and "the sound of water rushing in … within seconds, water was at chest level. The passageway leading to the ladder-well was blocked by debris, wires and other wreckage hanging from the overhead. From the light of the battle lanterns (the emergency lighting that turns on when there is a loss of normal lights due to power outage) he could see that he would have to climb over the debris to get to the ladder-well. As he started his climb across the debris to the open scuttle, the water was already within a foot of the overhead, so he took a breath, dove into the water, and swam towards the ladder-well. Underwater, he bumped into debris and had to feel his way along. He was able to stop twice for air as he swam, the water higher each time, and eventually used the pipes to guide him towards the light coming from the scuttle."

As he neared the exit, he was pulled out of the water by another sailor who had arrived to render assistance, his body "scraped, bruised, and covered with chemical burns from being submerged in the mixture of water and fuel." The sailors who had now gathered above the scuttle leading to berthing 5 faced the same harrowing decision as their counterparts on the *Fitzgerald* two months before. Inside the flooded compartment they knew their shipmates were trapped, but by that point the "green swirl of rising seawater and foaming fuel" was nearly at the level of the scuttle and threatened to sink the *McCain*. So, like on the *Fitz*, the sailors closed the scuttle, their hands slippery with water and fuel, and saved their ship.

Above berthing 5, many of the sailors inside berthing 3 were thrown out of their racks when the *Alnic* blew down a bulkhead and tossed racks, lockers, and other debris throughout the space. The panicked sailors were forced out as water and fuel began rising at their feet; they climbed over debris shifting inside the water and through loose, sparking cables hanging above, their bodies burning and slippery from the fuel. Because it was located mostly above the waterline, however, the space did not completely flood.

Closest to the point of impact, some of the sailors were trapped inside racks compressed by the crushed steel bulkheads (racks inside the berthing were stacked three on top of one another). As the two ships separated after being locked together, so did many of these racks, allowing sailors to escape. Two sailors, however, remained trapped in their beds. Sailors who had rushed down to berthing 3 to help heard their shouts and pried them out. The Navy report recounts one of these harrowing rescue efforts:

"The second Sailor was in a bottom rack in Berthing 3. His rack was lifted off the floor as a result of the collision, which likely prevented him from drowning in the rising water, and he was trapped at an angle between racks that had been pressed together. Light was visible through a hole in his rack and he could hear the water and smell the fuel beginning to fill Berthing 3. He attempted to push his way out of the rack, but every time he moved the space between the racks grew smaller and he was unable to escape. His foot was outside the rack and he could feel water. It was hot in the space and difficult to breathe, but he managed to shout for help and banged against the metal rack to get the attention of other Sailors in the berthing space. The Sailors who entered Berthing 3 to rescue others heard this and began assisting him, but he was pinned by more debris than the first Sailor freed. It took approximately an hour from the time of the collision to free the second Sailor from his rack. Rescuers used an axe to cut through the debris, a crowbar to pull the lockers apart piece by piece, and rigged a pulley to move a heavy locker in order to reach the Sailor. Throughout the long process, his rescuers assured him by touching his foot, which was still visible. Once freed, the Sailor was the last person to escape Berthing 3. Everything aft of his rack was a mass of twisted metal. He had scrapes and bruises all over his body, suffered a broken arm, and had hit his head. He was unsure whether he remained conscious throughout the rescue."

Throughout the ship, damage control teams battled the effects of flooding from the giant gash in the hull and from ruptured water pipes. Though their occupants had time to escape, multiple other berthings below the waterline aft of the ship were completely flooded as cracks caused by the impact allowed water to rush through. With ventilation inoperable, the temperature inside the ship became dangerously high and forced many sailors to take refuge on the flight deck. About an hour after the collision, as the crew isolated flooded compartments and continuously pumped out water, the *John S. McCain* slowly resumed her journey to Singapore, still the closest port. The USS *America*, an amphibious warship close by, sent Marine aircraft to assist in damage control efforts and to help treat the many injured sailors fighting through jagged steel, ripped electrical cables, and fuel. Along with Singaporean and Malaysian vessels, these aircraft also searched along the *McCain's* path for signs of her ten missing sailors. They did not find them.

McCain sailed the fifty remaining miles to Singapore at three knots. Though flooded compartments had been sealed, her captain had to be careful not to allow her damaged hull to let in any more water. Around noon that day, over six hours after the collision, the *McCain* finally entered Singapore and moored at Changi Naval Base. Navy divers immediately entered the water to access berthing 5. For the next seven days, they navigated through a dark mixture of fuel and seawater. Dodging floating debris and shredded metal, they were forced to cut holes through racks blocking their way. Inside were the bodies of ten sailors. They were:

– Nathan Findley, 31, Electronics Technician 1st Class, from Amazonia, Missouri

- Abraham Lopez, 39, Interior Communications Electrician 1st Class, from El Paso, Texas
- Kevin Sayer Bushell, 26, Electronics Technician 2nd Class, from Gaithersburg, Maryland
- Jacob Daniel Drake, 21, Electronics Technician 2nd Class, from Cable, Ohio
- Timothy Thomas Eckels Jr., 23, Information Systems Technician 2nd Class, from Manchester, Maryland
- Corey George Ingram, 28, Information Systems Technician 2nd Class, from Poughkeepsie, New York
- Dustin Louis Doyon, 26, Electronics Technician 3rd Class, from Suffield, Connecticut
- John Henry Hoagland III, 20, Electronics Technician 3rd Class, from Killeen, Texas
- Logan Stephen Palmer, 23, Interior Communications Electrician 3rd Class, from Decatur, Illinois
- Kenneth Aaron Smith, 22, Electronics Technician 3rd Class, from Cherry Hill, New Jersey

Two months after the tragedy of the USS *Fitzgerald*, we mourned the loss of ten more of our shipmates. Seventeen of the country's sailors had now died that summer. Once again, we found ourselves asking how an American warship had run into a merchant vessel in peacetime, and again, there were many sides to that answer. But just like on the *Fitz*, where the collision was most directly the result of poor training and negligence on the bridge, here too the causes pointed to a single glaring culprit. In this case, it was the very console that sailors on the *McCain* used to control their ship, the Integrated Bridge and Navigation System, or IBNS.

As the Navy's fleet of destroyers and cruisers approached or surpassed two decades of service, much of their navigation technology became woefully out of date when compared to the rest of the mariner industry. In 2011, the Navy hoped to solve that problem when it introduced the IBNS, a series of upgraded bridge systems that included touchscreen-only steering consoles and that would, over time, be retrofitted on all Navy ships. The *McCain* was the first ship to receive the upgrade in seventh fleet in 2016.

Despite the Navy's intentions, the IBNS touchscreens were clumsily designed, plagued by crowded displays where important information was difficult to locate, and where steering control was shifted through small dropdown menus. Considering steering consoles were operated by the most junior sailors on any crew, these were shockingly unintuitive. The *McCain's* captain himself, in fact, did not fully understand the IBNS console on his ship, and aside from the nearly brand-new helmsman on watch at the time of the collision, it turned out the lee helmsman controlling the speed and the boatswain's mate who first initiated the transfer of steering were not part of the ship's regular crew; they had transferred from the USS *Antietam* only a few months before, after *that* ship ran aground in Tokyo Bay (there is more to be said on the Navy's other high profile mishaps). The *Antietam*, a thirty-year-old cruiser, had an older and entirely different steering system.

In the fallout of the *McCain* tragedy, that boatswain's mate, a chief with a supervisory role among enlisted sailors on the crew, was charged with dereliction of duty for failing to train his watch standers, namely the young seamen who manned the helm on the bridge. Even he, however, had received only minimal training on a system that was not yet the standard on other ships. It is also likely that watch standers would have had to dim the screens' brightness at night; adjusting one's eyes to darkness is crucial on the bridge, where any light pollution prevents officers and lookouts from identifying the lights of other vessels miles away. It's not hard to imagine, then, how the enlisted men at the helm of the *McCain* that night, given their lack of training and the system's poor design, would have struggled with the situation they found themselves in.

As on the *Fitz*, however, the *McCain's* leadership is not entirely without blame for inadequately preparing their crew to respond to a steering casualty. In their report, the Navy singled out the captain for ordering the transfer of speed control to the other screen without first briefing his watch team on the bridge. From the accounts of the four minutes that it took the *McCain* to drift into the *Alnic*, it is unclear what the other watch standers on the bridge were doing or whether they understood what their captain had ordered. Though it is unfair to assume a ship's captain should brief every decision he makes on the bridge, the *McCain's* commanding officer clearly overestimated his sailors' training.

Perhaps the most damning thing we can say about the *McCain's* captain, however, is that he seemed to entirely lose situational awareness after the helmsman initially announced he had lost steering. On the bridge it's common to experience "tunnel vision" when things go wrong, to get sucked into a problem and forget everything else that's going on around you; it happens especially to more junior officers. But that's why captains show up on the bridge when their officers face difficult situations like entering the world's busiest strait. It's also partly why the Navy puts so many damn officers on the bridge in the first place, so that when things break or young sailors panic, enough people are there to keep their eyes out the window and still navigate the ship.

On the *McCain*, that didn't seem to happen. Nobody attempted to contact the *Alnic* on the radio or sound whistle blasts to alert the tanker they were careening toward her. It shouldn't have been a surprise they had just overtaken the *Alnic* and were now turning directly into her; their compass was still working, after all. As for the watch standers on the *Alnic*, they can hardly be blamed for not getting out of *McCain's* way. For one, they were required to maintain course and speed as a vessel being overtaken, according to the international navigation rules. More importantly, the debacle on the *McCain's* bridge only lasted four minutes; that's not a lot of time for a thirty-thousand-ton tanker to make a decisive change of her course or speed.

There is more to say about who is to "blame" for what happened on the USS *John S. McCain* and the USS *Fitzgerald*. That is perhaps a pointless question, or the most important one. First, one needs to understand how the Navy reacted to these two tragedies. One thing is for sure, though: the stories of the *Fitz* and the *McCain* aren't over.

CHAPTER 11

Postmortem

In the aftermath of the 2017 tragedies, the media struggled to come to terms with the most obvious question: *How?* How did accidents like these happen in the US military, our most hallowed and noble national institution? It was difficult, for one, to attribute blame. The average person doesn't exactly know the intricacies of the navigation rules of the road or how watch teams are composed aboard warships. The commanding officers of both ships were obvious targets, but terms like *officer of the deck* and *tactical action officer* were nonsense to the American public. Unsurprisingly, then, reports came out that one or both ships had possibly been "hacked" by foreign enemies. Suffice it to say, such claims were groundless and an absurd attempt to inject paranoia into very real tragedies.

Over the new few months, several crew members on both ships were charged with counts of negligence under the military justice system. Most notably, the officer of the deck of the *Fitzgerald* during the collision was taken to court-martial and pled guilty to dereliction of duty. She ultimately avoided criminal charges, received a letter of reprimand and was docked half her pay for three months. The Navy pursued charges of negligent homicide against the *Fitzgerald's* commanding officer, Bryce

Benson, and the tactical action officer on watch that night. These were later dropped and both officers were eventually allowed to transition out of the Navy under honorable conditions. Benson avoided even lesser counts of dereliction of duty in large part because it was determined that the chief of naval operations, in speaking out against him during the legal proceedings, had exercised "undue influence" on the case. Benson, in a rebuttal to the secretary of the Navy's letter of censure against him, maintained his innocence and contended that his ship and sailors had met the Navy's operating requirements.

The *McCain's* commanding officer, meanwhile, who was effectively heading the bridge watch team when the incident occurred, pled guilty to dereliction of duty and admitted to his part in the collision, namely for not posting enough watch standers for the navigational situation the ship was in at the time. He was allowed to retire with his current rank. The *McCain's* former chief boatswain's mate, however, who was responsible for training sailors to use the ship's steering console, was found guilty of the same offense and demoted one rank.

Navy leadership decided to go further. Only days after the *McCain* collision, they removed Vice Admiral Joseph Aucoin from his post as head of seventh fleet, in charge of all naval units operating in Asia, citing "a loss of confidence in his ability to command." Aucoin's role, however, had nothing to do with sailors' initial training. For that the secretary of the Navy chose a different culprit: Vice Admiral Thomas Rowden, the head of all naval surface forces and known colloquially in the Navy as the "SWO boss." Rowden was forced into early retirement and represented, along with Aucoin, the highest dismissals attributed to the events of 2017.

In October of 2017, a Navy panel released the decisive report on the matter, the *Comprehensive Review of Recent Surface Force Incidents*. At over 170 pages, its results were nothing we didn't already know among SWOs, though perhaps it raised the eyebrows of admirals far removed from life aboard warships. It found among the causes of the *Fitzgerald*, *McCain*, and other recent surface ship incidents, a pattern of poor seamanship, degraded watch standing, an "erosion of crew readiness" required for the high operational tempo of ships in Japan, a lack of standardization among ships' navigational systems, and poor management of operational risk across the fleet. It was a damning list—were ships in Japan doing *anything* right?

Most tellingly, the review questioned the quality of training for SWOs across the Navy. "The result," it explained, "is the development of our SWO corps lacks objective and consistent qualifying standards and knowledge." Among the "systemic" issues found, the report also targeted the Surface Navy's "can do culture." Under pressure from higher-ups, it contended, ships' captains were apt to ignore recommendations from their officers and push their crews further than what was operationally safe. This careful choice of words seemed to mask the undeniably toxic culture that had come to dominate the surface warfare community, one defined by stark careerism in wardrooms' upper echelons at the expense of sailors' well-being. The *Comprehensive Review* wasn't just concerned with the Navy's two most recent collisions. In fact, the Surface Navy seemed to be collecting accident reports at an impressive rate.

Only a month before the *Fitzgerald* incident, the cruiser USS *Lake Champlain* was operating with an aircraft carrier in the Sea of Japan. After reversing course to maintain position with the carrier, the *Lake Champlain's* watch standers realized they had turned onto the path of a fishing vessel and made a series of confused maneuvering decisions which, though the fishing vessel had remained on a constant course for the last hour, ended in collision. The damage to both vessels was minor, but the incident's fallout uncovered, in the actions of *Lake Champlain's* officers, a failure to follow basic navigation and watch standing principles and an inability to use available systems on the bridge. In January of that same year the USS *Antietam*, another cruiser operating in Japan, ran aground in Tokyo Bay during a disastrous anchorage attempt. Despite the presence of a conning officer, officer of the deck, navigator, and the ship's captain, the bridge team failed to plan for the strong wind and current and botched normal anchoring procedures, causing their ship to drift into shoal water over a hundred yards away from their intended location and strike bottom.

A few years before, the Navy saw several other high-profile accidents that foreshadowed the events of 2017. In 2012, the destroyer USS *Porter* was attempting to cross the congested traffic lanes near the Strait of Hormuz to continue her transit into the Persian Gulf. In complete darkness, her officers became disoriented by the mass of lights crossing their bow from both directions. The captain soon arrived on the bridge and entered into a confused conversation with his officer of the deck about how to navigate the daunting traffic before them. In their back-and-forth over course and speed decisions, both failed to realize a tanker was closing fast on their starboard bow. The captain immediately ordered a hard turn to the left and engines full ahead, much like the officer of the deck had done on the *Fitzgerald*, only to ram the *Porter's* starboard side directly into the other vessel, which had the right of way. Though the damage topside was disturbingly similar to the *Fitz*, the tanker did not have a bulbous bow prominent enough to puncture the hull below the waterline and no sailors were seriously hurt.

The events of the *Porter* collision were captured on an audio recorder on the bridge that night. It reveals a nervous, overwhelmed officer of the deck being harangued by a captain who is himself unable to cope with the situation unfolding in front of him and, in desperation, makes a series of disastrous maneuvering decisions. It's easy to imagine that a similar sense of chaos reigned on the bridge of the *John S. McCain* on that night in August of 2017. At the SWO training school in Newport, the audio was added to a full recreation of the collision in one of their virtual reality bridge simulators. The effect is chilling; I felt my heart sink in my chest when I experienced it for myself. "This is exactly how my first captain used to act on the bridge," I told one of my classmates in reference to Commander Pinckney. Many had similar stories. Our instructors used the accident to highlight how quickly one can entirely lose situational awareness on a ship. "When in doubt," they advised us, "slow down."

There were, amazingly, many more similar accidents in the years before *Fitz* and *McCain*. Just a year after the *Porter* collision, the USS *Guardian*, a small minesweeper, ran aground in the Philippines. The event is famous in the Navy not just for the utter ineptitude of the ship's navigator in plotting a course directly over a charted coral reef but in the incredible effort it took to extricate the *Guardian* from her predicament. It turned out the reef was part of a national park and was a UNESCO World Heritage Site. If you were going to run aground anywhere in the world, this was probably one of the worst places to do it. Navy rescue and salvage ships arrived and evacuated the *Guardian's* crew the next day. As engineers pondered how to free the doomed ship and waves pushed her further into the reef, the accident quickly turned into an ecological disaster. Because of the damage to both the ship and the reef, the Navy had no choice but to cut the *Guardian* into three pieces and lift them out separately. The process took over two months, and when it was completed, the US Navy had lost a multimillion-dollar warship due to a navigational error.

The Surface Navy's long string of recent accidents doesn't end there. I could, for example, detail how in 2009 the USS *Port Royal* ran aground in Hawaii only hours after leaving port, and how hordes of tourists saw an American cruiser listing helplessly over the shallows as they flew into Honolulu's airport, but by now I think you get the point. *Fitzgerald* and *McCain* were not isolated events. They exemplified the culmination of years of ineptitude among the surface warfare community: a lack of knowledge about navigation, seamanship, and the systems aboard our ships. Shortly after the *McCain* accident, a headline from the *Navy Times*, the most ubiquitous news source focused on the maritime services, put it more bluntly: "Maybe today's Navy is just not very good at driving ships." This wasn't an exaggeration—what the hell was going on in the US Navy?

To answer that question, we have to go back to 2003. In an effort to cut costs in the face of an impending war, the Navy eliminated the six-month SWO Basic School which, at the time, all new surface officers attended in Newport before reporting to their first ship. The replacement? A set of twenty-one CDs issued to newly commissioned officers so they could teach *themselves* the finer points of navigation and driving ships. The Navy had entered the digital age; what need was there for instructors? This ridiculous system was derided by those who experienced it as "SWOS in a box," after the school in Newport, and was, as one former Navy captain and ship handling instructor put it, the "death knell of professional SWO culture in the United States Navy." My own department heads had lived through the program themselves and were among the first generations of naval officers whose grasp of the mariner profession was beginning to erode.

Expecting officers to learn the art of taking ships out to sea on their own was not just impractical, it was utterly stupid. Near the end of 2012 the Navy ended the experiment and reinstated initial training for SWOs in Newport, except this time it was a nine-week program called Basic Division Officer Course, or BDOC, which I attended as an ensign in 2015. Unfortunately, BDOC wasn't exactly focused on being a mariner either, and only dedicated about two weeks to navigation and seamanship. It offered a handful of sessions in virtual reality simulators, but these were aimed at learning basic conning orders, not at managing the complex navigational situations a mariner can encounter at sea. The remaining weeks concerned topics as far-reaching as ships' engineering plants, Navy administration, and the military justice system. BDOC maintained our community's stubborn insistence that SWOs should know a little about everything and, consequently, be experts at nothing.

The environment instilled at SWOS in Newport, one which squashes a professional training model in favor of PowerPoint presentations, reigns supreme on board our warships. Today, surface warfare officers are not trained as professional mariners. After nearly two decades of eroding training and qualification standards, the requisite knowledge and skills to competently take ships out to sea are nearly gone in the surface warfare community. This isn't a secret among SWOs, and worse, it's not like Navy leaders weren't warned before 2017. For years, in fact, high-ranked officials had stressed the difficulties facing the fleet to the very top of the chain of command.

In 2010, retired vice admiral Phillip Balisle conducted a sobering review of the state of the surface force. In his subsequent report, Balisle found, among other troubling signs, that ships' material readiness was below operational requirements, manning was overstretched, the shipboard qualification system was broken, and officer training was in decline. "The level of knowledge of newly reporting officers is lacking," the report stated. "There is a surplus of ensigns assigned to each ship which challenges the capacity of the senior officers and chief petty officers to train them. DDG's are mustering approximately 32 officers where ten years ago they mustered 21." The number of new officers was further preventing these ensigns from gaining ship handling experience. "The true impact of this situation," the report continues, "may manifest itself in a few years when the officers return to sea as Department Heads." This was the generation of department heads who became my immediate superiors during my tours as a division officer, and who led officers on board the *McCain* and *Fitzgerald* in 2017.

In 2012, Navy Undersecretary Robert Work took notice of these mounting problems. He sent rounds of data to then-deputy secretary of defense, Ash Carter, who later became secretary of defense in the two years before the collisions, showing that the fleet was overtaxed. His concerns were largely ignored. The following year, Vice Admiral Thomas Copeman, then "SWO boss" and head of all naval surface forces, warned that readiness was headed in a "downward spiral" at a Surface Navy symposium. Copeman claimed the comments drew harsh criticism from the staff of the chief of naval operations. In August, he issued memos highlighting lack of training among sailors and how differing interfaces for ships' equipment would lead to confusion, problems that came to a head during the *McCain* incident in particular. Copeman was replaced in 2014. Two years later, a new Navy undersecretary, Janine Davidson, expressed the same concerns as her predecessor to Ray Mabus, the secretary of the navy and highest official in the Navy's administrative chain of command. She later claimed that Mabus, who served from 2009 to January of 2017, was focused primarily on shipbuilding and increasing the size of the fleet during his tenure, and ignored pleas to prioritize sailors' readiness. In a later interview, Mabus assumed no responsibility for the collisions of 2017. "Both of them were failures on those ships," he stated, and called the fact that they came within weeks of each other "a coincidence."

Then there's Joseph Aucoin, the former head of seventh fleet who was sacked immediately following the *McCain* collision. Aucoin had been a career Navy aviator who, now in charge of the operation of all naval units in Asia, had no direct ability to influence the manning of his ships or the training of his sailors. It's not like he ignored these issues, however. In February of 2017, four months before the *Fitzgerald* incident, he presented data about his ships' declining readiness to his immediate superior and head of the entire Pacific Fleet. No action was taken in response. Throughout that year, the paranoia surrounding the North Korean missile threat only further taxed overworked ships in Japan. Meanwhile, as Aucoin struggled to draw attention to a problem he couldn't fix on his own, the vice chief of naval operations testified to Congress in February that the Navy was in "top shape."

After retiring from the Navy, Aucoin defended himself in a 2018 article by pointing to the Navy's refusal to accept overall "organizational responsibility" for the tragedies. "I do not understand," he wrote, "why our leaders do not push back on the excessive demand on our ships or exhibit more transparency on the true extent of the issues the Navy faces beyond Seventh Fleet." Indeed, Aucoin had emphasized the gaps in manning and training but had received no support from his superiors. Ships in Japan, he noted, were especially undermanned and strained by the heaviest operational cycle in the Navy, which caused sailors to be temporarily loaned from one ship to another, and which in turn resulted in a lack of knowledge about ships' systems from sailors standing watch on those ships.

Aucoin also addressed the particular crisis facing the SWO community. "I think the main culprit for these collisions," he wrote, "was that we allowed the training of our surface warriors to atrophy." Of the many issues highlighted by the Navy's investigations of the collisions, the most pressing was "the near-constant reorganization of SWO Division Officer formalized training, wherein greater reliance on PowerPoint instruction and on-the-job training have been ascendant (in contrast to submarine, flight, and SEAL training and at the Marine Corps Basic School). Our Surface navy is loaded with talent and great people, but they have lacked some of the foundational building blocks of training that have been eroded or simply cut because of budgetary pressure." He added that the USS *Porter* accident in 2012 had already made this problem clear, but hadn't compelled Navy leaders to act. He questioned, after many more subsequent incidents, "whether we truly have the resolve to *fix* these issues for our surface warriors."

Vice Admiral Aucoin's last plea barely registered in our wardrooms. Instead, we quietly got back to work. No commanding officer was going to admit that the *Fitzgerald* incident could be reproduced on *their* ship. Yet one would hope that, in the Navy's highest echelons, the tragedies of 2017 were the wake-up call needed to address the elephant in the room. So what have Navy leaders done since then?

After *McCain*, then chief of naval operations, Admiral John Richardson, ordered a one-day "operational pause" for all ships. Lacking substance, the move simply highlighted the problem without offering a common solution. In classic Navy fashion, a slew of administrative demands came in its wake: more stringent casualty report procedures, an updated navigation instruction, new guidelines for ship's standing orders, and a new task force to certify ships in the Pacific Fleet. These essentially took what the Navy was already doing and did more of it.

Some meaningful measures were taken, however. All ships were directed to adopt a circadian rhythm for watch standing, which consisted of shorter, more frequent watches designed to facilitate a healthier sleep routine for sailors. Indeed, the system was almost universally preferred to the brutal "five-and-dime" rotation we had experienced on the *Carney*. The Navy also standardized watch team structures and called for more lookouts on ships while underway. This requirement proved double-edged; though more eyes on watch is not a bad thing, it required more sailors to be on watch at sea to begin with and has added to the general level of fatigue among crews on deployment.

Vice Admiral Rowden, before being ousted, also mandated Navy-wide ship inspections, dubbed *Ready for Sea Assessments*, starting with forward-deployed ships in Japan. RFSA, as it was known, became a rehash of the fleet's existing navigation certification system, and enforced administration inspections, rules of the road exams, and basic navigation drills, all identical to measures that were already a part of ships' regular training cycles. The only difference was that RFSA was administered directly by fleet representatives, as opposed to individual squadrons and the Navy's laughably ineffective certification authority, the Afloat Training Group. The whole program was essentially a way for admirals to say, "we don't trust what our commodores and captains are doing, so we're going to do the same thing ourselves."

Navy leaders did manage a more tangible initiative alongside RFSA; between January and March of 2018, assessors from the SWO training command carried out "competency checks" on a random selection of newly qualified officers of the deck across the fleet. Testing these officers' ability to react to real-life situations in ship simulators, the Navy found that, out of the 164 tested, only 27 passed with "no concern." The rest, SWOs trusted by their commanding officers to lead bridge teams and navigate the ship on their own, were found deficient in the basics: using radars, applying navigation rules of the road, and reacting effectively in dangerous situations.

The most decisive action to improve SWO training was the development of a junior officer of the deck course for surface officers. As of 2019, newly commissioned ensigns now get four weeks of simulator training focused on basic mariner skills and ship driving immediately after BDOC. This is welcome news, but it's not nearly enough. Even the officer of the deck on the USS *Fitzgerald*, before she ran headfirst into a thirty-thousand-ton cargo ship, was a second tour division officer with hundreds of hours of bridge watch under her belt. And on the USS *Porter*, both a lieutenant department head and the commanding officer were present on the bridge. Four weeks of simulator sessions won't change the fact that SWOs aren't formally trained mariners.

The Navy also started issuing "mariner skills logbooks" to all surface officers to record hours spent on watch, a standard in the mariner and aviation industries. The intent is to ensure officers get more time at sea, but so far there has been no indication of how these will be used and no change in how officers become qualified to stand watch on the bridge. Officers of the deck are still made not through a standardized process, but haphazardly aboard their ships. This is central to the SWO crisis, and because of the Navy's entrenched on-the-job qualification system, it's not likely to change anytime soon.

I became intimately familiar with many of these efforts, since I became the navigator of a littoral combat ship, the USS *Coronado,* after the summer of 2017 and was responsible for administering RFSA and every other newly imagined navigation initiative. How did actual SWOs serving in the fleet, far away from admirals, respond to these solutions? To be honest, they barely registered. That's because the Surface Navy rolled them out piecemeal, and though taken together our leaders could claim they were solving the problem, as individual efforts they were lackluster at best. These weren't the answers we had hoped for. They were Band-Aids.

Imagine the Surface Navy as one great ship. Now imagine there is a glaring hole on the bottom of that ship and water is rushing in, and the ship is slowly sinking. The Navy's response since 2017, in concocting many small solutions for many small problems, is akin to running around the ship looking for other leaks, and when one is found, plugging it up with oakum and duct tape. Then, when someone points out the big hole in the hull, they say, "But look! We've been plugging a lot of holes and the ship is not taking on as much water!" Sure, that's not wrong, but down below there's still a big hole, and it needs to be fixed.

Navy leaders haven't fixed that glaring hole, the one that is causing so many accidents on board Navy ships. It's not like we're the only organization that drives ships out in the ocean, after all. In all these accidents, the pattern is unmistakable: Officers standing watch on the bridge are making mistakes. What we need, rather than a few additional weeks of simulator time, is an entirely new training model for surface warfare officers in the Navy. One way to do that is to look at what everybody else is doing.

CHAPTER 12
Troubled Waters

In my deployments in Europe, I spent a great deal of time with the Royal Navy, both during FOST and the many NATO exercises the *Carney* participated in. In my interactions with the Brits, I became convinced of their superior training model, one in which officers spend months in school and at sea learning the mariner's craft before worrying about leading divisions. More than that, the Royal Navy fosters a completely different attitude about their surface officer corps when compared to their Yankee counterpart. For one, they designate a separate community entirely dedicated to engineering, officers who do not concern themselves with navigation and standing watch on the bridge.

This is so intuitive that after five years of active-duty service in the Navy, it's utterly baffling to me that we don't do the same. Running a ship's engineering plant requires a particular kind of expertise and knowledge, and engineering mishaps, even more than navigation, are the most widespread type of accidents in the Surface Navy. Yet engineering officers on board Navy ships, other than nuclear reactor officers serving on aircraft carriers, receive almost no formal training in their job, and are expected, while overseeing the most dangerous equipment on board, to act as mariners and stand watch on the bridge. We don't ask pilots to oversee the maintenance of their aircraft, so why do we ask SWOs to balance two professions that both require their complete attention?

The Royal Navy's "warfare officers," who are initially trained as mariners, are held to the kind of professional standard we expect out of aviators or submarine officers in the US Navy. Officer hopefuls in flight training or nuclear reactor school regularly fail, and attrition is accepted as a necessary part of their training pipelines. Not only is there a lack of professional standards in the SWO community, but dropouts from the aviation or submarine programs often end up as surface officers, a phenomenon that has contributed to the SWO community's reputation for amateurism in the Navy. SWOs' role as mariners, however, is every bit as important to our national defense as that of jet pilots or infantry officers.

When I went to navigator school in Newport, a chief petty officer remarked, "I don't understand how you guys spend four years at Annapolis and aren't navigation experts by the time you're done." I hadn't gone to the Naval Academy, but he had a point, though he failed to realize that the academy's purpose was to grant college degrees, not to create mariners or pilots. SWOs, to this day, lack the equivalent of the UK Royal Naval College. Our training hub in Newport is made up largely of Navy lieutenants who, though they purport to be experts at navigation and seamanship, are themselves the product of a substandard training system.

Why can't the Navy simply stand up a new, more rigorous training pipeline for SWOs? It would take time and considerable resources, to be sure, and might require the Navy to seek help from outside its own ranks. Most importantly, creating a new generation of surface officers takes *will*, exactly the kind of will that Vice Admiral Aucoin alluded to and doubted our current Navy leadership could muster up. That would require those very leaders, who head our squadrons, fleets and training commands, to admit the shortcomings of their own profession, and that a better, more competent generation of officers can replace them.

It's more than just a money problem; the surface warfare community must surmount an enormous cultural obstacle before anything can change for good. SWOs today do not see themselves as mariners but as *generalists*. That's why when I stepped into a Navy recruiting office for the first time, the lieutenant aviator behind the desk couldn't even explain what a SWO was and why, predictably, he tried in vain to steer me in another direction. The "generalist" concept assumes that surface warfare officers, as they advance in rank and eventually become commanding officers of ships, are better off knowing a little about everything rather than specializing in any one thing, be it engineering, communications, navigation, or warfighting. That's why officers' shipboard qualifications comprise every imaginable naval topic and why we are randomly placed into divisions as ensigns. Most captains, in fact, believe it is better for officers to lead more than one division throughout their first tour, and preferably in completely different departments.

Being a mariner, ironically, is not a profession in the US Navy. It's part of being a SWO, but a SWO can just as well be an engineer, an administrator, or a cybersecurity manager. "Division officer" and "bridge watch stander" have become almost interchangeable roles even though the two have nothing to do with one another. Many have justified the generalist model by asserting that it results in more talented and versatile commanding officers of ships. That's a judicious answer; too bad it's complete bullshit.

The first lesson I learned in leadership, before I even stepped into the *Carney's* radio room for the first time, was to *"know your job."* Sailors, I found out, will trust you until you give them a reason *not* to, and nothing will obliterate those sailors' respect for their chiefs and officers faster than someone who doesn't know what they're talking about. Sailors are proud of their professions; many tattoo their rating insignias on their arm or on the top of their hand. So when a new boss shows up who doesn't know what's going on in their division or who has never worked on their equipment before, those sailors understandably become bitter and are forced to ask a simple question: Other than the rank on your collar, why should I listen to *you*? I've seen many leaders, both officers and enlisted, fail spectacularly for that reason.

Does the Navy's SWO model make better commanding officers? Maybe, but at what expense? They're not the ones standing watch on the bridge or running divisions. What matters in an organization as complex and unwieldy as the Surface Navy is talented, knowledgeable sailors and leaders, and officers don't make good leaders if they're not experts at what they do. It's not fair to hand a binder full of qualifications to a young ensign reporting to their first ship, put them in charge of real sailors and real equipment, and wish them well. Asking senior enlisted chiefs to train officers is also misguided. Chiefs don't have that much time to devote to their DIVOs, and the hierarchy of rank is turned upside down if the subordinates must hold their superiors' hand through their job.

By now, the generalist culture is deeply and stubbornly entrenched in our wardrooms. It is rare to see senior officers question it; rather it is the model on which they have based their careers. In their eyes, SWOs are generalists and the better you are at being a generalist, the better you are at being a SWO. But that mentality hurts sailors most of all, because it creates officers who are more interested in their careers than at being good at their jobs and, in turn, doing right by their sailors. It also contributes to the toxic culture of micromanagement that runs rampant aboard our ships, the "Master Tickler" brand of leadership that seeks to crush everything in sight with paperwork and Excel spreadsheets. The Navy needs professional mariners, not bureaucrats.

Perhaps I've gone too far and, as sailors like to say, I'm getting *twisted around the shaft*. Let's go back to the USS *Fitzgerald* and the USS *John S. McCain*. I'm not sure if we've answered the question a lot of Americans asked themselves in the summer of 2017, the one about who is to blame. Unfortunately, it doesn't have a straightforward answer.

Without a doubt, the captains of both ships at the time must shoulder some of that blame. When naval officers take command of a ship, they accept responsibility for everything that happens on board. It's called the burden of command, and it's why, in exchange, they are treated as *lord paramount* by their sailors. On the *Fitzgerald*, the officer of the deck who took charge of the bridge that night must also accept her part in the collision. Though we may point to fatigue and deficiencies in her training, she was still an officer and she was not standing a proper watch. Did those individuals deserve harsher punishments? No—the guilt they live with to this day is undoubtedly enough.

What about everyone else? It's hard to say whether Vice Admiral Aucoin, the former head of seventh fleet, was purely a scapegoat for the Navy. One thing is for sure—he was not a SWO, and was certainly not responsible for the deficiencies in surface officer training aboard the ships under his command. These deficiencies were, I hope I've made clear, the primary reason for these tragedies. In their own investigation of the *McCain* collision, the National Transportation Safety Board concluded that the probable cause for the accident was "a lack of effective operational oversight of the destroyer by the US Navy, which resulted in insufficient training and inadequate bridge operating procedures."

At the very top of the Navy hierarchy stands the service's highest-ranked officer, the chief of naval operations, or CNO, and above him a civilian official appointed by the president, the secretary of the Navy. Together, they lead the Navy's administrative chain of command and have three missions: *man, train, and equip.* In other words, they recruit sailors to the Navy, train those sailors, and ensure they are equipped to do their job *before* they deploy to operational fleets.

In the eight years immediately preceding the collisions, the Navy saw three different CNOs, two of which were trained as submariners. Is any one of them *more* responsible for failing the SWO community? With so much turnover at the top, it's hard to say who was in charge of the Navy leading up to 2017. Ray Mabus, the secretary of the Navy during those same eight years, simply shrugged off all blame for the incidents. Some things did remain consistent: a lack of attention, despite repeated warnings, to sailors' readiness to take ships out to sea, and an insistence on building more ships at the expense of training and manning. It is unfortunate that the sweep of dismissals that followed the *McCain* incident, and which saw the removal of two three-star admirals, did not extend to the two highest posts in the Navy, the chief of naval operations and the secretary of the Navy, despite the fact that it was these individuals who had the most influence, and with it the most responsibility, to effect change in their organization.

It will take time to see whether the SWO community's small solutions since 2017 can solve its major crisis. In May of 2020, then-secretary of the Navy, Kenneth Braithwaite, commented that "failings of leadership" had put the entire Navy department in "troubled waters." Among other recent controversies, he noted that the collisions were "indicative of a breakdown in the trust of those leading the service." Since Ray Mabus left the office in January of 2017 to today, seven other individuals have occupied the post of secretary of the Navy. Indeed, the confidence among sailors that the Navy can solve its own problems is exceptionally low. Among surface warfare officers, there is a widespread conviction that our community is plagued by dysfunctions and is in need of serious reform. Perhaps my first department head, Lieutenant Masker, was right. Instead of flashing a light in every corner and feigning shock at what we find, maybe we should just turn on the lights.

Conclusion

In August of 2017, after a few weeks in Rhode Island, I traveled to Naval Base San Diego to begin my second tour as the navigator of the littoral combat ship USS *Coronado*. For the next three years, I toiled aboard one of the most disastrous class of ships to ever be commissioned in the US Navy, one which, since its inception in 2008, has been plagued by endless controversy. The *Coronado*, a three-thousand-ton aluminum trimaran, had barely enough weapons to call herself a warship, and broke down so often that every time we took the bridge to get her underway, it was just as likely we would not be able to leave the pier for some catastrophic equipment failure. On one occasion, *Coronado's* propulsion lost all power in the middle of San Diego Bay and we were forced to lower her anchor to prevent the ship from running aground. As we waited for the tugboats to tow us back to the pier, we drifted helplessly and in full view of the aircraft carriers moored inside the ship's namesake city of Coronado.

The USS *Coronado* was kept afloat only through the unimaginable resilience of her crew. Inside her wardroom, and despite the ship's radical design, the same SWO culture as on the *Carney* reigned supreme: unshakable institutional thinking, a nearly Kafkaesque level of bureaucracy, and a captain whose delusions sometimes rivaled Commander Pinckney. If there was any question that the surface warfare community's problems were endemic, it was confirmed during my time in San Diego.

As I neared the end of my active-duty service, however, I could not help but admit my undeniable gratitude toward the Navy, an organization that had taken me from New England to Florida, along the shores of Europe and North Africa, and finally to Southern California. The Navy had entrusted me with a level of responsibility and leadership unheard of for inexperienced young men and women in the civilian world. Despite all the frustration, it had forged out of me something of a mariner and allowed me, just like I had dreamed, to drive warships out to sea. To be sure, this is a challenging time in the Navy's history, but certainly not one without a solution. As one of my shipmates once remarked, "We defeated the Nazis and the Japanese Empire at sea in only a few years, surely we can figure *this* out."

The day I stepped off the brow of a Navy warship for the last time, it was pouring torrents of rain, not a common occurrence in San Diego. I asked one of my fellow officers to take a photo of me on the pier, in front of the *Coronado*. Despite my drenched uniform, I did my best to appear composed. Five years earlier, in Mayport, Florida, another officer had taken a nearly identical picture of me in front of the USS *Carney*, albeit a bit younger and without a SWO pin.

Then, just like that, I was done with shipboard life. No more days on duty and hours spent standing at the quarterdeck with a pistol strapped to my hip. No more nights on the bridge, eyes fixed on the darkness and the occasional lights of other vessels on the horizon. No more Sundays grilling hamburgers on the flight deck or mooring at faraway ports. No more complaining to one another inside the JO Jungle or sitting through interminable briefs inside the wardroom. No more "aye, sir" and talk of decks, bulkheads, forward and aft and port and starboard. No more 2 a.m. conversations with the ITs, the cooks, the engineers, the operations specialists, the quartermasters, and the many other young men and women who make up a ship's crew.

Mostly, I was glad I hadn't listened to my recruiter.

Sailors have a favorite saying to make sense of the Navy's hardships, one made up of only three words: *ship, shipmate, self.* Every sailor learns it as they step aboard their first command, a guide for how to comport themselves in the hallowed organization they now find themselves in. It's meant as a hierarchy for what they should prioritize, in that order. The organization is first, the individual last. It makes sense—most sailors are barely out of high school when they enlist, and they have to understand that, in the military, it's not about them anymore. Those three words serve as a common axiom for Navy leaders, be it a chief who commands a handful of sailors or a captain who commands the crew of an aircraft carrier. It justifies everything we do in the Navy: the working weekends, the nights on watch, the long months at sea, and the years missing your kids' birthdays.

I don't take fault with those three words, only their order. The ships are not the priority in the Navy. The sailors are. Ships aren't always reliable. They rust, they break often, and, most importantly, they are useless by themselves. Maybe one day we will figure out how to make ships that don't need sailors. Why not? Like I said, being out to sea mostly sucks, but we're far from automated destroyers, and a ship is still only as good as the people who run her radars, engines, and networks, and who stand watch on her bridge and deep inside her plant.

If the Navy continues to focus more on machines than people, I don't think that will ever change. The sailors, the individuals who make up the organization, are its most valuable asset. And when we neglect their training and their well-being, those people make mistakes, and sometimes we pay for those mistakes in lives. The only individuals who can change that are those at the top of the organization, the officers who command our ships, our squadrons, and our fleets. They're the ones who set the tone for how we do business in the Navy. Our problem is not one of money, it's one of *culture*, and before the culture of the Surface Navy can change, the culture of the *wardroom* must change. That's the place where officers eat and hold meetings and make the rules for everyone else.

One of the first things I learned as an officer was to own the mistakes my sailors made. It's time the Navy's leaders do the same.

References

ARTICLES

Paris, Jon. "The Status Quo Killed 17 US Sailors. The Navy Must Change." Defense One, May 31, 2018. https://www.defenseone.com/ideas/2018/05/status-quo-killed-17-sailors-us-navy-must-change/148625/

Ziezulewicz, Geoff. "Worse than you thought: inside the secret Fitzgerald probe the Navy doesn't want you to read." Navy Times, January 13, 2019. https://www.navytimes.com/news/your-navy/2019/01/14/worse-than-you-thought-inside-the-secret-fitzgerald-probe-the-navy-doesnt-want-you-to-read/

Ziezulewicz, Geoff. "The ghost in the Fitz's machine: why a doomed warship's crew never saw the vessel that hit it." Navy Times, January 14, 2019. https://www.navytimes.com/news/your-navy/2019/01/14/the-ghost-in-the-fitzs-machine-why-a-doomed-warships-crew-never-saw-the-vessel-that-hit-it/

Faram, Mark. "Maybe today's Navy is just not very good at driving ships." Navy Times, August 27, 2017. https://www.navytimes.com/news/your-navy/2017/08/27/navy-swos-a-culture-in-crisis/

Ziezulewicz, Geoff. "A warship doomed by 'confusion, indecision, and ultimately panic' on the bridge." Navy Times, January 14, 2019. https://www.navytimes.com/news/your-navy/2019/01/14/a-warship-doomed-by-confusion-indecision-and-ultimately-panic-on-the-bridge/

Faturechi, Robert, Megan Rose, and T. Christian Miller. "Years of Warning, then Death and Disaster: How the Navy failed its sailors." ProPublica, February 7, 2019. https://features.propublica.org/navy-accidents/us-navy-crashes-japan-cause-mccain/

Miller, T. Christian, Megan Rose, and Robert Faturechi. "Fight the Ship: Death and valor on a warship doomed by its own Navy." ProPublica, February 6, 2019. https://features.propublica.org/navy-accidents/uss-fitzgerald-destroyer-crash-crystal/

Miller, T. Christian, Megan Rose, Robert Faturechi, and Agnes Chang. "Collision Course." ProPublica, December 20, 2019. https://features.propublica.org/navy-uss-mccain-crash/navy-installed-touch-screen-steering-ten-sailors-paid-with-their-lives/

Aucoin, Joseph. "It's Not Just the Forward Deployed." Proceedings, US Naval Institute, April 2018. https://www.usni.org/magazines/proceedings/2018/april/its-not-just-forward-deployed

Larter, David B. "Troubling US Navy review finds widespread shortfalls in basic seamanship." Defense News, June 6, 2018. https://www.defensenews.com/naval/2018/06/06/troubling-us-navy-review-finds-widespread-shortfalls-in-basic-seamanship/

Paris, Jon. "The Virtue of Being a Generalist, Part 3: Viper and the Pitfalls of 'Good Enough.'" Center for International Maritime Security, August 19, 2014. https://cimsec.org/virtue-generalist-part-3-viper-pitfalls-good-enough/

"SECNAV Nominee Braithwaite Written Statements to SASC." USNI News, May 7, 2020. https://news.usni.org/2020/05/07/secnav-nominee-braithwaite-written-statements-to-sasc

Faram, Mark. "The Navy is ready to dump the military's most pointless uniform." Navy Times, April 23, 2016. https://www.navytimes.com/news/

your-navy/2016/04/23/the-navy-is-ready-to-dump-the-military-s-most-pointless-uniform/

"NWU under fire: Report raises concerns." Military Times, March 20, 2013. https://www.militarytimes.com/2013/03/21/nwu-under-fire-report-raises-concerns/

Werner, Ben. "Marine Corps Suicide Rate Declines, Navy Rate Rises in 2019." USNI News, February 6, 2020. https://news.usni.org/2020/02/06/marine-corps-suicide-rate-declines-navy-rate-rises-in-2019

Phillips, Dave. "Three Suicides in One Navy Ship's Crew Point to a Growing Problem." New York Times, September 24, 2019.

OFFICIAL REPORTS

Report on the Collision between USS FITZGERALD (DDG 62) and Motor Vessel ACX CRYSTAL. Washington, D.C.: Department of the Navy, 2017.

Report on the Collision between USS JOHN S MCCAIN (DDG 56) and Motor Vessel ALNIC MC. Washington, D.C.: Department of the Navy, 2017.

Supplemental Preliminary Inquiry and Line of Duty Determination Regarding Injuries and the Deaths of Seven Sailors Aboard USS Fitzgerald (DDG 62) on or about 17 June 2017. Department of the Navy, 2017.

Strategic Readiness Review: 2017. Department of the Navy, 2017.

Comprehensive Review of Recent Surface Force Incidents. Norfolk, VA: Department of the Navy, 2017.

Marine Accident Investigation Report. Japan Transport Safety Board, 2019.

Marine Accident Report: Collision between US Navy Destroyer John S. McCain and Tanker Alnic MC, Singapore Strait, 5 miles northeast of Horsburgh Lighthouse. Washington, D.C.: National Transportation Safety

Board, 2017.

Balisle, Phillip M. *Fleet Review Panel of Surface Force Readiness.* Department of the Navy, 2010.

Readiness Reform Oversight Committee. Washington, D.C.: Department of the Navy, 2019.

Lightning Source UK Ltd.
Milton Keynes UK
UKHW020645281022
411251UK00015B/797

9 781953 321206